Contents

Introduction

When I began working on this book I had one fact clear in my mind—diagrams are far more easily understood than descriptions. It is for this reason that the book is set out in this way. There are many pattern-cutting books on the market that are available to the student of fashion, but I felt that a fresh approach to the subject was necessary in order that the subject could become more easily comprehensible and therefore more enjoyable.

Our book has been written not with any particular sector of readers in mind as I feel it could easily be used by all who are interested in the subject—whether a Diploma student, a Certificate student, or a dressmaker at home. It covers all the basic steps of dart manipulation and garment styling, as well as the more advanced topics such as tailored collars and coats.

All the work enclosed should be simply used as a guide, and gradually, as confidence and ability is gained, it should be interpreted in your own personal way—in other words, you will be designing patterns, not simply drafting them.

I hope that the reader finds this book a helpful aid which will continue to be a source of inspiration.

Acknowledgments

I would like to thank Mrs Mary Bromly, the Head of the Fashion Department at Newcastle Polytechnic, and my fellow members of staff, in particular Miss Dorothy Anderson, for their help in the writing of this book.

Hilary Campbell

Adapted to suit Australian standards
by Michael Stuart Davies, T.T.R.I.C., D.T.T.,
Melbourne College of Textiles.

Producing a Pattern

Designing Patterns

As fashions change the ideal body size and shape also changes; we have only to look back a few decades to see a variety of fashionable silhouettes, from the shapeless, flat-chested 'flapper' of the twenties to the small waisted, shapely New Look of the late forties. The pattern-cutter has to be aware of this fact and continually be changing the basic blocks from which he or she works. Although the majority of today's women wear little underwear or corsetry the pattern-cutter should always be aware of the nature of what is worn and how, if at all, does it affect the outline of the body to be fitted.

The Standards Association of Australia continually releases tables of measurements in order to reflect the size and proportion of the women of the day. Different clothing firms aim at particular markets, a fact which often influences their selection of measurements.

After the basic techniques of flat pattern drafting have been mastered, the use of calico modelling on stands may also be introduced; either to test the flat patterns or by modelling directly on to the stand. Ideally both methods should be used in conjunction with each other to achieve the best results.

Pattern-cutting Requirements

The following items are required to enable the cutter to create clear, correct and accurate patterns:

Good quality white pattern paper

Large sheets or roll of cardboard (for basic blocks)

A Perspex square with 45° and 90° markings as well as centimetre measurements

A 15 cm plastic ruler (useful for marking seam allowances)

A pair of sharp paper cutting scissors

A good-quality tape measure (with metal ends)

Clear sticky tape

A soft rubber

3H or 4H pencils (no softer) and pencil sharpener

Dressmaker's pins

Fine felt pens (to outline parts of draft)

A metre stick

A tracing wheel would also be found useful, as would a dressmaker's stand.

A calculator

Although 'french curves' are an easy method of drawing curved lines, it is far better to achieve the skill of freehand drawing which comes with practice.

Points to note when Pattern Cutting

1. When measuring curves use the tape measure on its edge.

2. Accurate, clear lines are essential, and these can only be achieved with the use of hard sharp pencils; sharpened with a pencil sharpener, not a knife. Sketchy lines have no place in pattern cutting.

3. Notches are almost always marked at 90° to the seam line on which they are placed.

4. The two sides of a dart must always be identical in length.

5. Grain lines are marked parallel to the CF or CB except in a few cases, for instance a flared panel in a skirt would have the grain line marked through its centre as in a sleeve.

6. Calico is available in varying weights and qualities, so whenever possible use the type most similar to the fabric chosen for your garment to test your pattern.

7. If the pattern is to be used on a fabric with a nap, i.e. corduroy, mark grain line in normal position but have the 'arrows' facing in one direction—usually upwards.

Seam Allowance Guide

Seam allowance	Light-weight or medium-weight fabric	Heavy-weight or bulky fabric
0.5 – 1 cm	Collars, neck lines, sleeveless arm holes, facings or any enclosed seam	Impracticable
1.5 cm	Side seams, shoulder seams and waist seams	Collars, neck lines, sleeveless arm holes, facings or any enclosed seam
2 cm	Side seams, waist seams and any seam possibly requiring alteration	Side seams, shoulder seams and waist seams
2.5 cm	Hem allowance on very flared skirts and seams possibly requiring alteration	Side seams, waist seams and any seam possibly requiring alteration
5 cm	Possibly hem allowance	Hem on flared coats or skirts
6 – 8 cm	Usually impracticable	Possible hem allowance on coats

Basic Draft

1. Select relevant basic cardboard blocks of the required size suitable for your design.

2. On a pencil line drawn at 90° to the edge of the paper, line up the blocks on the chest line or hip line, depending on which block is being used, with the side seams facing inwards. The CB and CF lines will now be parallel.

3. Draw in any style lines, change dart positioning, add allowances for fastening etc. to achieve your selected design.

4. Before tracing off all the pattern pieces check your basic draft thoroughly; seam lengths, grain lines, facings, notch positions, fastenings, etc. Every detail must be marked on to this draft, and under no circumstances is it to be cut into as it should be retained with the final pattern pieces for reference.

Pattern Pieces

1. Carefully trace off each separate section of the pattern, ensuring that pieces are cut on the fold of paper when necessary (do not write on 'place on fold'). Grain lines, balance notches and all other relevant details must be transferred.

2. Seam allowances are now added; the amount of the seam allowance used varies considerably depending on position, the garment style and the fabric to be used. See Seam Allowance Guide table on the opposite page.

3. The following information must be marked on each pattern piece:

Grain line	Number of pieces to be cut
Balance notches	Amount of seam allowance used
Size of pattern	CF or CB line when applicable
Name of pattern piece	Your own name

Examples of Correctly Marked Pattern Pieces

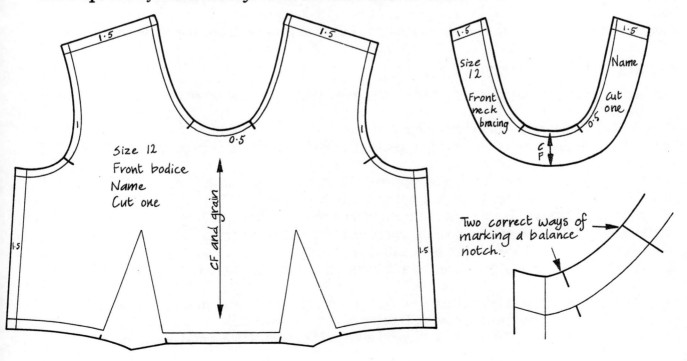

Two correct ways of marking a balance notch.

3

Metric Sizing Chart

Size		8	10	12	14	16
				Average Women		
To fit bust	cm	75	80	85	90	95
To fit waist	cm	55	60	65	70	75
To fit hip	cm	80	85	90	95	100
Girth measurements (cm)						
Neck-base		35	36	37	38	39
Thigh (maximum)		46	50	53	56	59
Knee		31	32	34	35	36
Upper arm		23	24	26	28	29
Lenths and widths (cm)						
Nape to waist		38	39	39.5	40	40
Waist to hip/seat		17	18	18	20	20
Crutch/body rise		26	27	27	28	28
Across back		30	31	32	33	34
Across chest		29	30	30	31	32
Bust point to bust point, across		17	17.5	18	18	18.5
Waist to hip		19.5	20.5	21	21.5	22
Shoulder length		11	11	11	11.5	11.5
Waist length, front		33	34	34	35	35
Waist length, back		38	39	39	40	40
Arm length, shoulder to wrist		58	58	59	60	60
Underarm length		42	43	43	43	43
Height	cm	160	161	163	164	165

Measurements—where and how to take them

Take all measurements closely but not tightly.

All vertical measurements should be taken on one side only.

All horizontal measurements should be taken with the tape measure parallel to the floor except in the case of the chest measurement when it finds its own level according to the figure. Measure the figure over the undergarments to be worn beneath the finished garment.

Bodice Measurements

1. BUST – Around fullest part of bust, ensuring tape measure does not slip down at the back.
2. WAIST – Around natural waist line.
3. HIPS – Around fullest part of hips, generally over the bottom, approx. 20 cm below waist line.
4. UPPER HIPS – Around hip bones, approx. 10 cm below waist line.
5. BACK LENGTH – From nape (back of neck) to waist line.
6. FRONT LENGTH – From base of throat to natural waist line.
7. BACK WIDTH – From arm hole to arm hole, about half-way down.
8. CHEST – Around body, above bust and under arms.
9. HIGH CHEST – From arm hole to arm hole on the front, approx. 10 cm below base of throat.
10. SHOULDER – From neck point to point at which arm begins and shoulder finishes.
11. SCYE DEPTH – From nape, down CB to lowest level of arm hole.
12. SCYE CIRCUMFERENCE – Around arm hole, whilst arm is in normal position.

Where to take Measurements

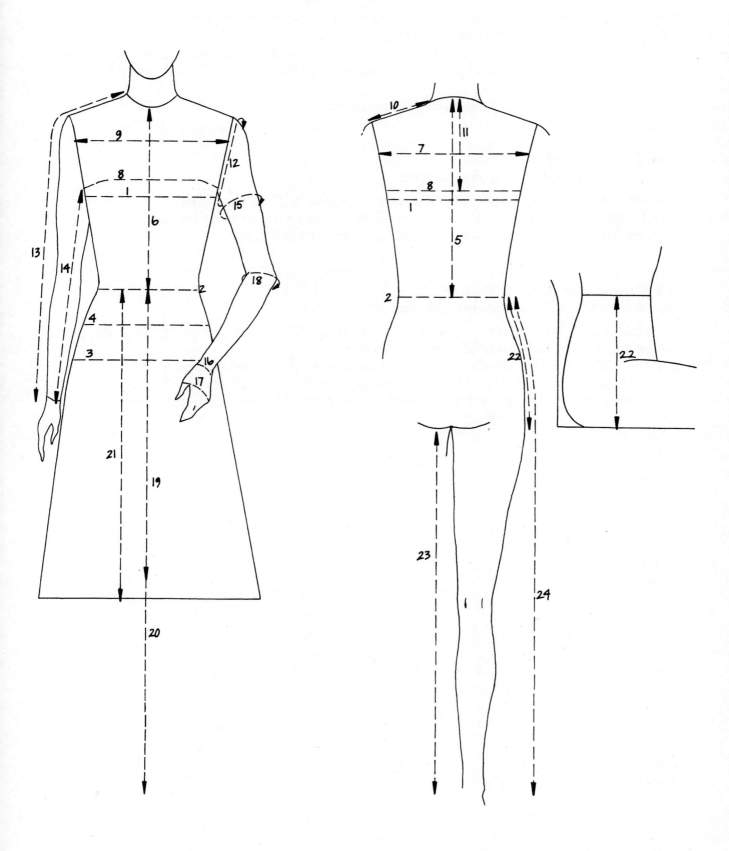

Sleeve Measurements

13. **NECK TO WRIST LENGTH** – From side of neck, along shoulder, down arm to wrist; allow tape measure to follow curve of arm.
14. **UNDER ARM LENGTH** – From under arm to wrist.
15. **BICEP** – Around widest part of upper arm, high under the armpit.
16. **WRIST** – Around widest part of wrist.
17. **HAND WIDTH** – Around widest part of hand; this measurement enables the cutter to make the wrist of the sleeve wide enough to pass over the hand if there is to be no opening.
18. **ELBOW WIDTH** – Around elbow with arm bent.

Skirt Measurements
(in addition to waist and hip measurements)

19. **WAIST TO KNEE LENGTH** – From waist line, down CF, to knee level.
20. **WAIST TO ANKLE LENGTH** – From waist line, down CF to ankle level.
21. **SKIRT LENGTH** – From waist line to length of skirt required.

Trouser Measurements
(in addition to waist and hip measurements)

22. **BODY RISE** – From waist line, down to seat of chair, over contour of hips; the person should be seated on a solid and upright seat.
23. **INSIDE LEG LENGTH** – Down from crutch to level of outside ankle bone.
24. **OUTSIDE LEG LENGTH** – Down from waist, over hips to ankle bone. The actual length of trousers will vary depending on fashion; these last two measurements are only a guide.

The Bodice – Part One

Bodice Block

Scale

This block is created with the use of a scale factor, to ensure that proportions are correct whatever size is drafted. The standard chest measurement of 76 cm forms the basis of a simple calculation. This standard chest measurement is added to the actual chest measurement of the required size, and then divided by 2. This gives an average chest measurement. As we construct blocks to represent half of the body we only need to use half of this measurement.

Example: size 12

$$\frac{76\ cm + 80\ cm}{2} = \frac{156\ cm}{2} = 78\ cm$$

78 cm = Average measurement
39 cm = Scale (half average)

Measurements – Size 12

Bust = 85 cm
Chest = 80 cm
Nape to waist = 39.5 cm
Shoulder = 11 cm
Half across back = 16 cm

Drafting Instructions

Bodice Block

    2 from 1 = nape to waist measurement
    3 from 1 = quarter scale
    4 from 1 = half scale plus 2.5 cm
    5 from 1 = half bust and tolerance allowance of 5 cm; square to points 6 and 7
    8 from 4 = one third chest plus 1 cm tolerance
    9 from 4 = half across back measurement plus 1 cm tolerance 10 is midway 8 and 9;
              square up to 11 and 12
   13 from 1 = one tenth scale plus 3 cm
   14 from 13 = 1.5 cm draw in a smooth line from 14 to 1
              join 14 to 15 with a dotted line
   16 from 14 = shoulder measurement plus 1.5 cm dart allowance plus 1 cm tolerance
   17 from 16 = 1 cm
   18 from 3 = one fifth scale plus 3.5 cm draw in a 1.5 cm dart from mid shoulder to 18
   19 from 5 = one fifth scale minus 1.5 cm
   20 from 19 = 1.5 cm (add 5 mm for every 2.5 cm over size 12 bust) join 20 to 3 with a dotted
              line
   21 from 20 = one fifth scale plus 1 cm draw in neckline
   22 from 12 = one fifth scale
   23 from 20 = shoulder measurement plus 1 cm tolerance plus dart allowance (=19 to 22)
   24 from 23 = 1.5 cm
   25 from 8 = 1.5 cm, square across to centre front line
            26 = is midway 25 and the centre front
   27 from 4 = one fifth scale plus 3 cm
            28 = is midway 20 and 24
   29 from 28 = half bust dart allowance (19–22)
   30 from 28 = half bust dart allowance
              join 29 and 30 to point 26
   31 from 7 = 2 cm contour allowance, connect to point 2

Dart Distribution

Back waist dart: 2.5 cm to be positioned on a line squared down from point 27.
Front waist dart: 4.5 cm to be positioned on a line squared down from point 26.
Side seams: 2.5 cm on either side of a line squared down from point 10.

Completing Draft

1. Draw in the arm hole shape, making curve deeper at the front.
2. Fold out back and front shoulder darts. Connect 14 to 17 and 20 to 24 with ruled lines.
3. Fold out waist darts, place side seams together, and connect 2 to 31 with a good curved line, ensuring that angles at CF and CB waist and neck line are 90°.

Bodice Block

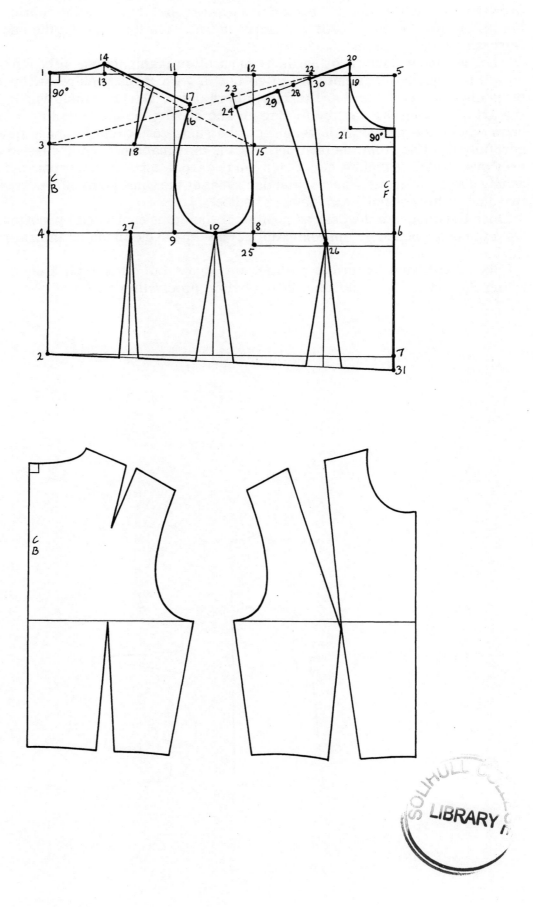

9

Darts

Darts are used to enable a flat piece of fabric to fit a three-dimensional human figure. In our basic bodice draft there are two darts in the front in order to shape the fabric successfully over the bust, whilst the two back darts are required to shape the fabric over the shoulder blades. As the shoulder blade is a fairly smooth area the darts on the back need only to be fairly small and do not meet at any point.

The two front darts are the darts most often manipulated, although any dart may be moved if required. It is not very often that a garment is required with the darts in their original positions as there are so many alternatives. 'Dart manipulation' is the term used for the art of moving the dart by folding up and closing the unwanted dart area and slashing open where the new dart is required. The same result can be more quickly obtained by carefully pivoting from the bust point. If the dart manipulation is carried out correctly the previous good fit is maintained. Often the two front darts are incorporated into one, but this is only possible because the original darts met at the same point; it is not possible to combine two darts if they do not, as in the back bodice.

Once the dart is in the desired position it should be shortened by moving outwards, away from the prominence by approximately 2 cm; thus avoiding an unnatural pointed area over the bust.

Take off the final pattern as outlined on page 3, cut out sample from calico for personal fitting. Adjust block to personal fitting before proceeding further.

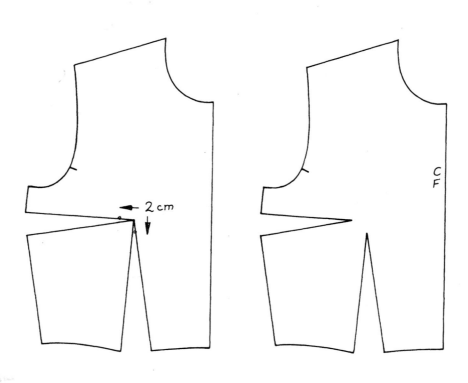

Six Examples of Dart Positions

(Shaded areas move whilst remainder stays the same.)

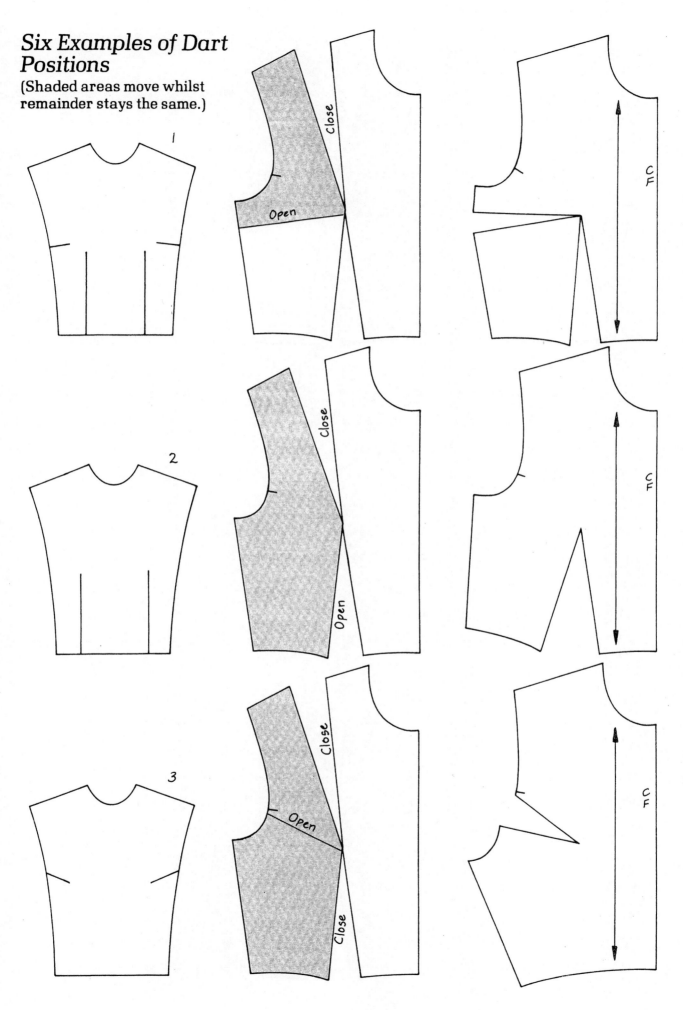

11

Shaded areas move whilst
remainder stays the same.

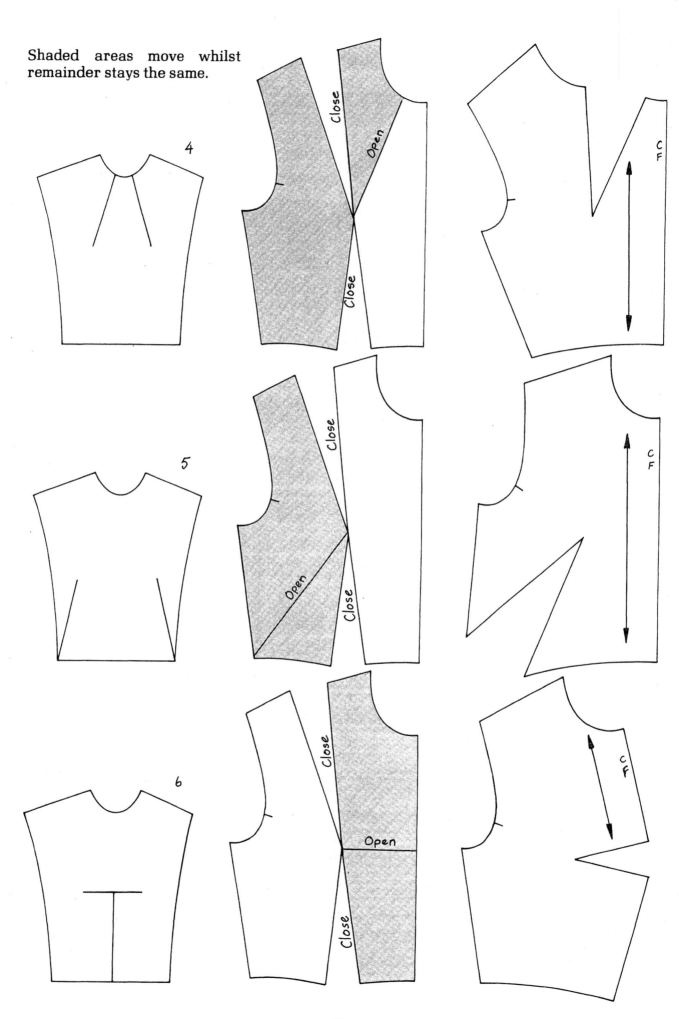

Shaped Darts

1. *Square Darts*

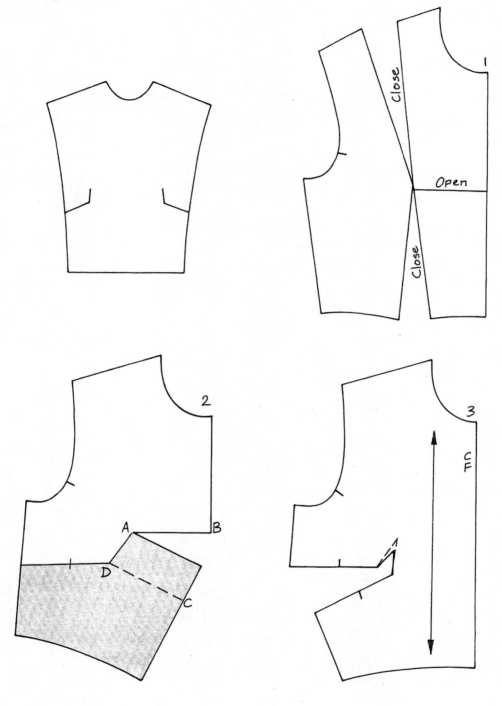

1. Swing both darts into CF.
2. Draw in shaped dart line and mark in notch. A–D should not be less than 6 cm in length. D–C = A–B + 2 cm.
3. Trace off lower section and close front dart; this will open up the shaped dart at side seam. Shorten dart by 2 cm.
   Seam allowance must be added to the dart as it is stitched up as a small seam, not as a folded dart.

2. Curved Darts

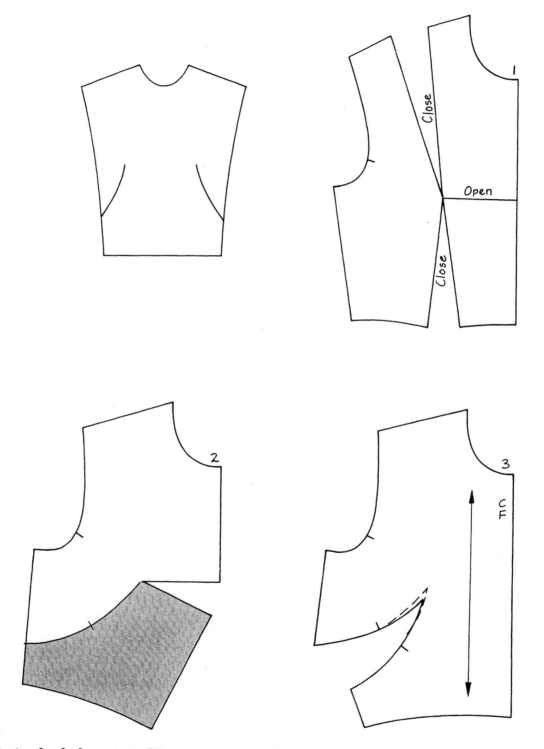

1. Swing both darts into CF.
2. Draw in curved dart line and mark in notch.
3. Trace off lower section and close front dart; this will open up the shaped dart at side seam. Shorten dart by 2 cm.
   Seam allowances must be added to the dart as it is stitched up as a seam, not as a folded dart.

The Back Shoulder Dart

The back shoulder dart is usually left in its original position on the basic bodice block but sometimes it may be necessary to remove it if it is interfering with the garment design. Here are three suggestions if this is the case.

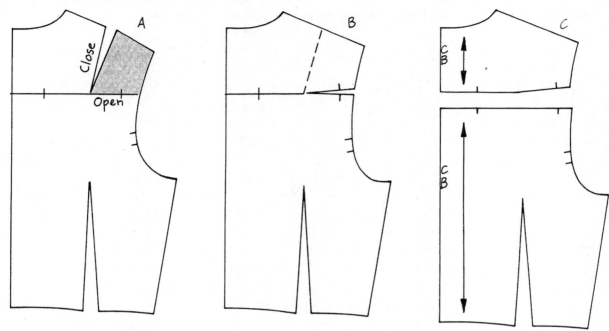

1. Yoke Styling

A. Draw in yoke shape touching end of dart, mark in two notches.
B. Trace off yoke section closing dart.
C. When the two sections are stitched together the garment will fit as well as with the original dart.

3. Eased Shoulder Seam

Draw a straight line from neck line to shoulder; the fullness of the dart is now eased into the front shoulder seam.

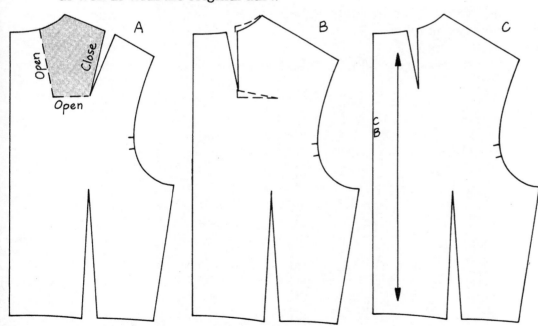

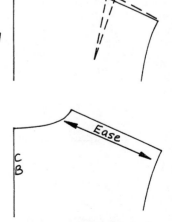

2. Transferring to Neck

A. Trace off shaded area and close shoulder dart.
B. Ensure that both sides of new dart are equal; smooth off neck line.
C. When the neck dart is stitched the shoulder area remains straight.

This is only suitable for fabrics that ease well.

Bodice Styles

1.

1. Measure neck line and swing volume of both darts into it.
2. Fullness is gathered up to measure original neck line measurement.

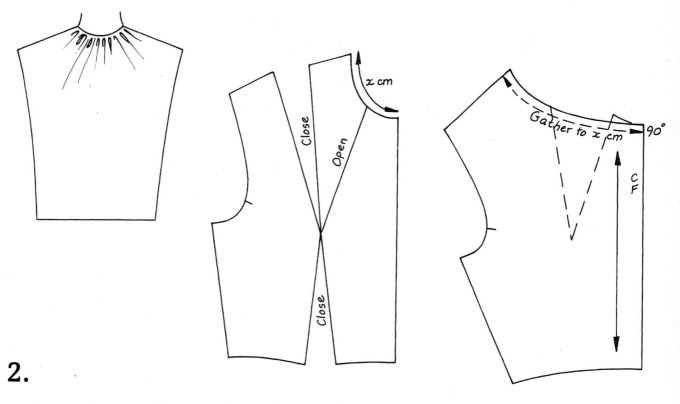

2.

1. Lower front neck line. Notch CF where gathering detail is to be positioned and measure distance between these two notches.
2. Swing volume of both darts into CF.
3. Fullness is gathered up to measure original notched measurement.

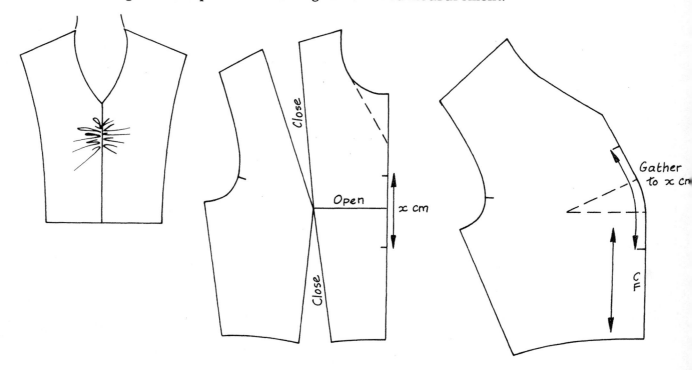

3.

1. Swing both darts into neck line.
2. Extend CF upwards; draw a line from shoulder to meet extended CF at 90° angle.

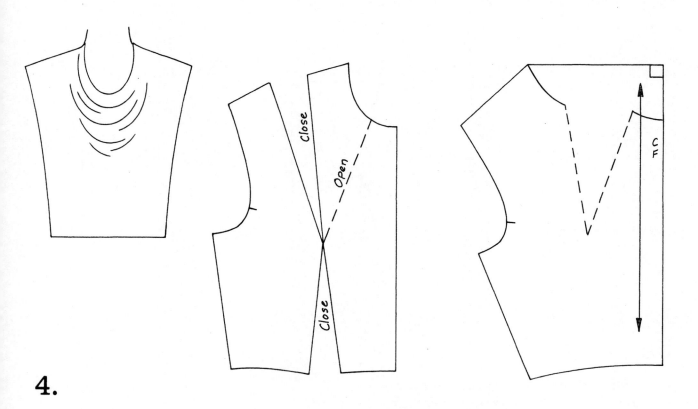

4.

1. Lower front neck line; draw in side panel and notch.
2. Trace off side panel and swing both darts into new position where it now forms soft gathers.

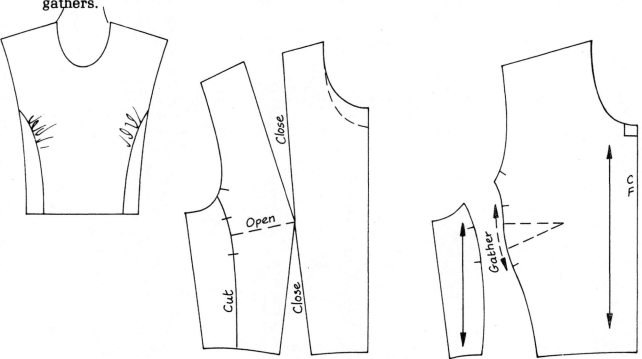

5.

1. Swing shoulder dart into waist dart.
2. Draw in yoke shape and position notches.
3. Trace off main body section and swing volume of dart into seam line, where it now forms soft gathers.

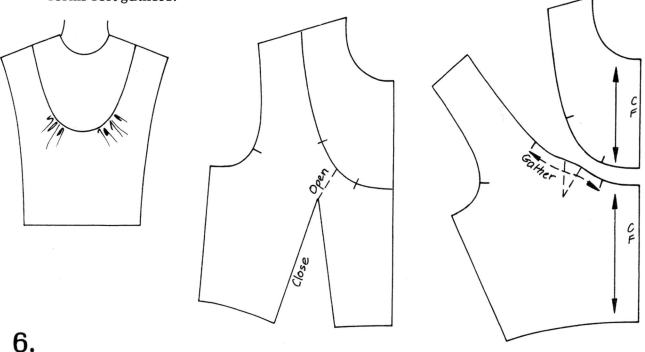

6.

1. Swing waist dart into shoulder dart.
2. Draw in style line and position notches.
3. Swing volume of shoulder dart into seam line.
4. Midriff panel is cut open and the top edge overlapped 1 cm to ensure a close fit to the body.

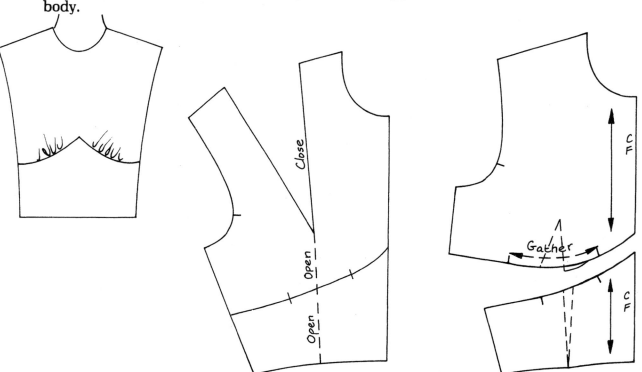

7.

1. Swing shoulder dart into waist dart.
2. Mark cutting lines on side section and open on each line to give shape as diagram; smooth off edge to give a smooth curve.

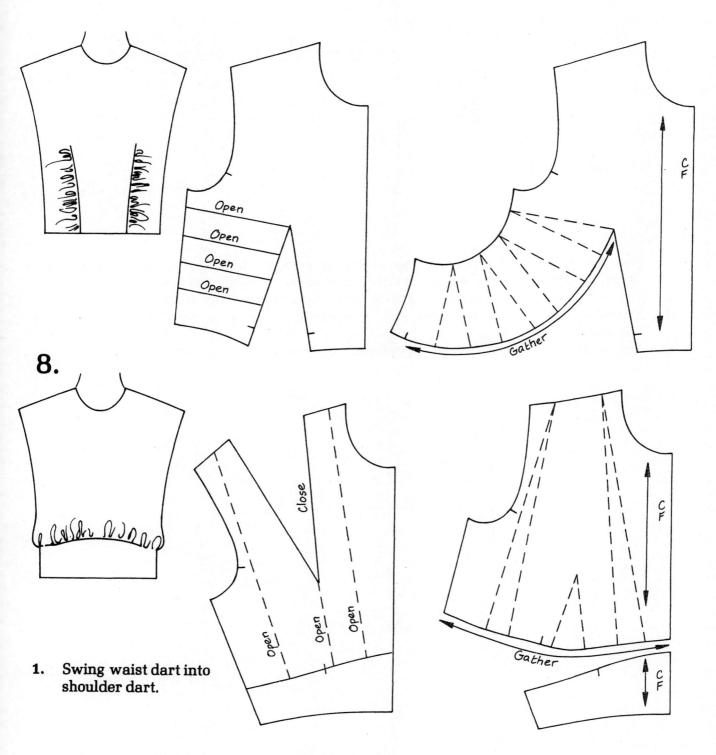

8.

1. Swing waist dart into shoulder dart.

2. Draw in waist panel and mark in three cutting lines.
3. Close shoulder dart and open up bodice at lower edge, keeping shoulder points together.

9.

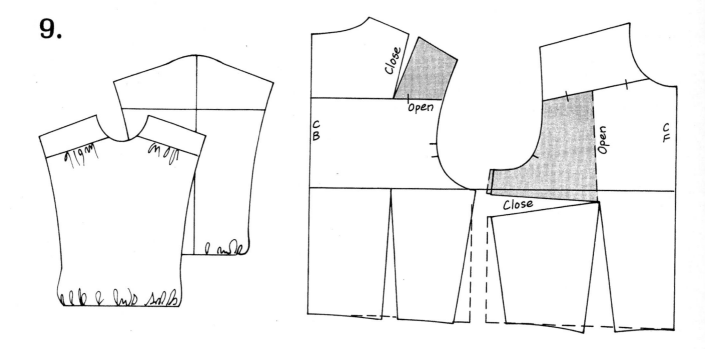

1. Line up bodice blocks on chest line, swinging front shoulder dart temporarily into side seam. We forget about waist darts as they are now left as fullness at waist.
2. Draw in yoke lines and mark in notches; add 2.5 cm to side seam at waist line.
3. Trace off front and back yokes and incorporate into one pattern piece by joining at shoulder.
4. Swing volume of side dart into original position, where it now forms soft gathers.

10.

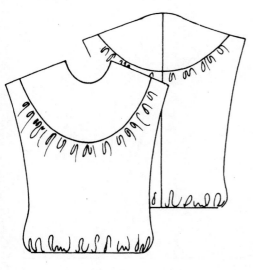

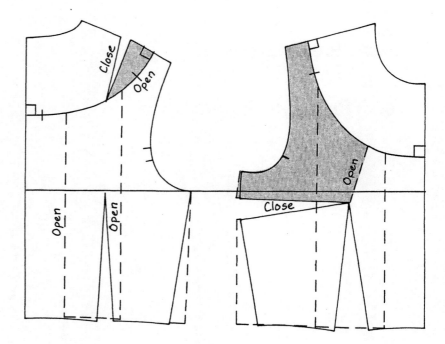

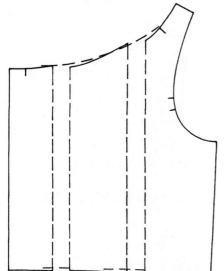

1. Line up blocks on chest line, swinging front shoulder dart temporarily into side seam.
2. Draw in curved yoke lines and mark in notches. Add 2.5 cm to side seam at waist line.
3. Mark in cutting lines on front and back bodices. Front and back waist darts are left unstitched to give extra fullness at waist.
4. Trace off shaded areas and redraw new positions on draft. Trace off the three sections on the front and back where cutting lines are positioned, and open up to give fullness. Trace off these new front and back shapes and the two yoke pieces.

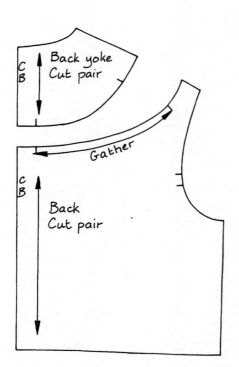

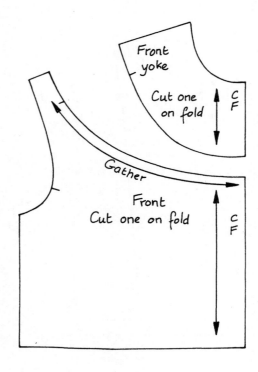

21

Panelled Bodices

1. *Princess Style Bodice*

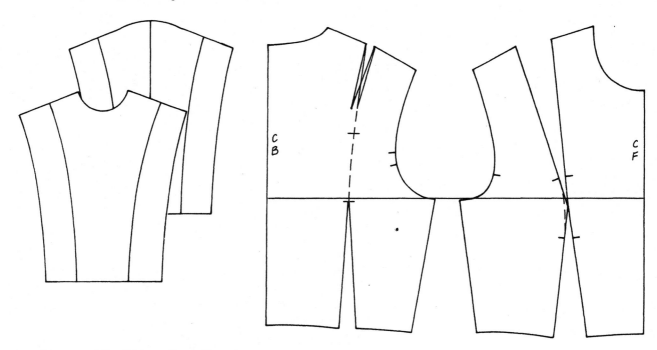

1. Line up blocks on chest line.
2. Divide front and back bodices with smooth seam lines; adjust position of base of back shoulder dart if necessary, to achieve a good line.
3. Position notches and trace off each panel marking grain lines parallel to CF and CB.

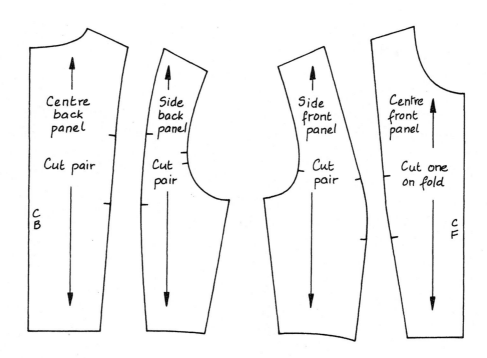

2. Wing Seamed Bodice

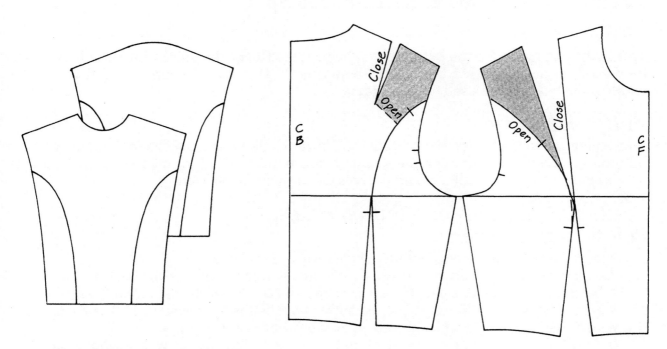

1. Line up blocks on chest line.
2. Divide front and back bodices with smooth curved seam lines; position notches.
3. Swing back shoulder dart into seam line and mark as ease; swing front shoulder dart into seam line; these shaded areas should be traced off and added on to the main sections in order to close darts accurately.
4. Trace off each panel after marking grain lines parallel to CF and CB.

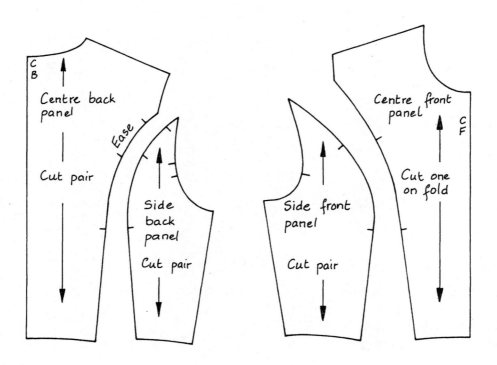

The Bodice – Part Two

Positioning Buttons and Button Holes

Button Wrap

This is the term used for the extension made past the CF, or the point where the button is to be placed, to accommodate button and button hole. The button wrap is usually made the width of the button to be used (left diagram).

Button Hole Size

To accommodate the button comfortably the button hole must measure the diameter of the button plus 0.3 cm to allow for the shank of the button. An allowance of up to 1 cm may occasionally be necessary if a particularly large button is to be used.

Positioning Buttons and Button Holes
Points to remember:

1. Wherever possible place a button at bust level to avoid gaping.
2. A button must be placed at the breakpoint, on a garment with a revers collar.
3. A button at the neck line should be positioned a button's width down from the neck edge.
4. A button is essential at waist line except when a belt is to be worn with the garment, in which case a button must be placed equally on either side of the belt.
5. Button holes are usually placed at right angles to the button wrap, where they are strongest, but in the case of a placket fastening the button holes must lie down the centre, vertically. The 0.3 cm extra allowance is marked above the button whilst the width of the button is marked below.

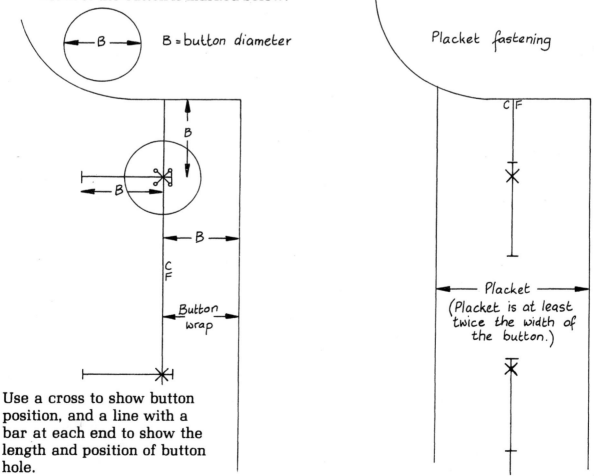

B = button diameter

Placket fastening

Button wrap

C F

Placket
(Placket is at least twice the width of the button.)

Use a cross to show button position, and a line with a bar at each end to show the length and position of button hole.

Plackets

1. *Placket for Reversible Fabrics*

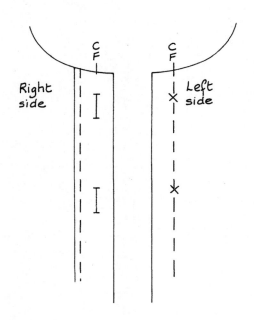

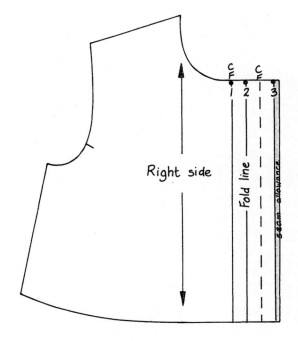

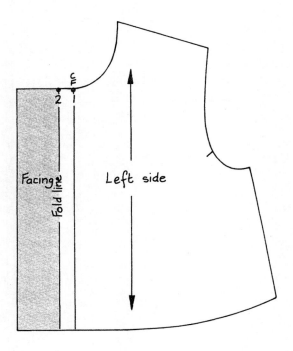

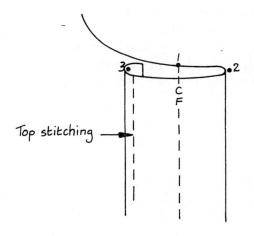

1–2 = Half width of placket.

2–3 = Width of placket.

The left side of the garment does not usually have a placket but simply a corresponding button wrap and facing.

2. Placket for Non-reversible Fabrics and Garments with Yokes

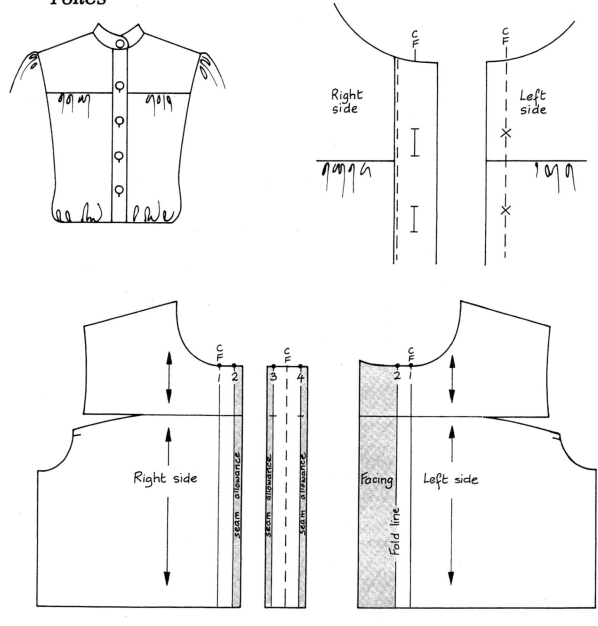

Right side

Left side

Right side   seam allowance   seam allowance   seam allowance

Facing   Fold line   Left side

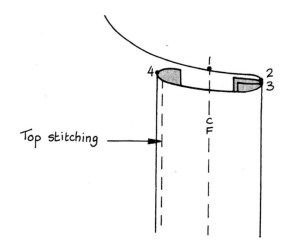

Top stitching

1–2 = Half width of placket.
3–4 = Width of placket.
The left side of the garment does not usually have a placket but simply a corresponding button wrap and facing.

3. Short Placket

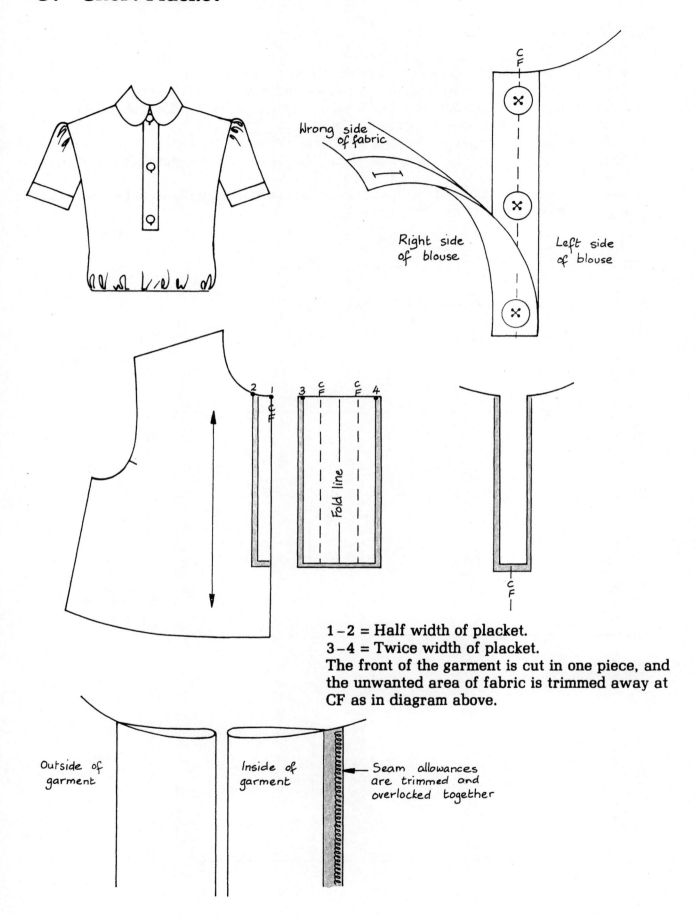

Wrong side of fabric

Right side of blouse

Left side of blouse

Fold line

1 – 2 = Half width of placket.
3 – 4 = Twice width of placket.
The front of the garment is cut in one piece, and the unwanted area of fabric is trimmed away at CF as in diagram above.

Outside of garment

Inside of garment

Seam allowances are trimmed and overlocked together

Neck Line Shaping

Points to remember

1. Front and back neck lines do not have to be lowered the same amount.
2. Front and back neck lines must be widened the same amount.
3. On a garment with a collar it is not advisable to either widen or lower the back neck line; if the garment is to be worn over another it is only necessary to widen the front and back neck line slightly as well as lowering the front.
4. It is advisable not to try to construct a literally 'square' neck line as it is rarely successful. The sides of the neck line should be gently curved outwards towards the shoulder.
5. After any alterations have been made check that neck line continues to be a smooth line at shoulder where front and back meet.

Examples

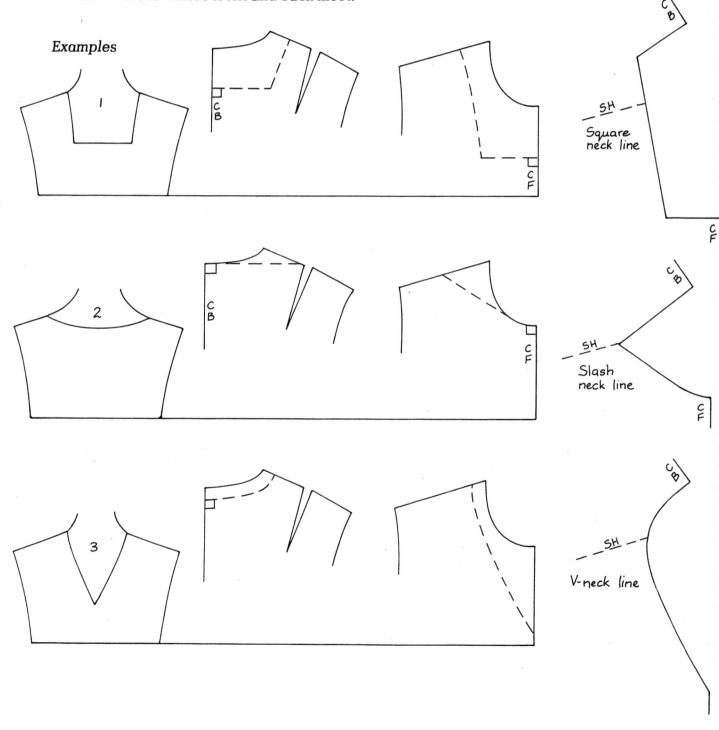

Square neck line

Slash neck line

V-neck line

28

Facings

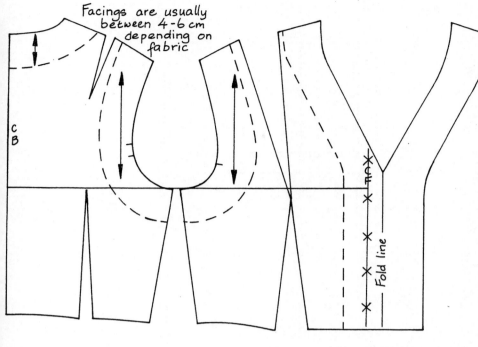

Facings are usually between 4-6 cm depending on fabric

A facing is required at collarless neck lines (as well as with certain collars), sleeveless arm holes, and edges that are fastened with buttons. In the diagram on the left there are separate facings at the arm hole and back neck line, whilst the front edge, which fastens with buttons, has a grown-on facing; this is preferable to a separate facing as a seam down the front edge is avoided. The grain lines should be marked on the basic draft (parallel to CF and CB) before being traced off.

The example below shows the arm hole and neck line facings in one. On a garment where the arm holes and neck line are cut away, ordinary separate facings would overlap each other giving unwanted thicknesses of fabric, so the arm hole and neck line facings are incorporated into one. Once the shape is determined mark in a horizontal line on to the facing and slash on vertical line; keeping guide lines level overlap the two sections to lose 0.5 cm. This prevents the facing being visible when attached.

To avoid a seam at the shoulder the front and back arm hole facings may be cut together with original shoulder seam notched.

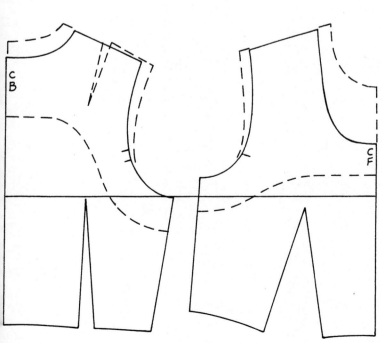

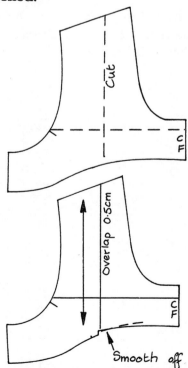

Pockets

Simple Patch Pockets

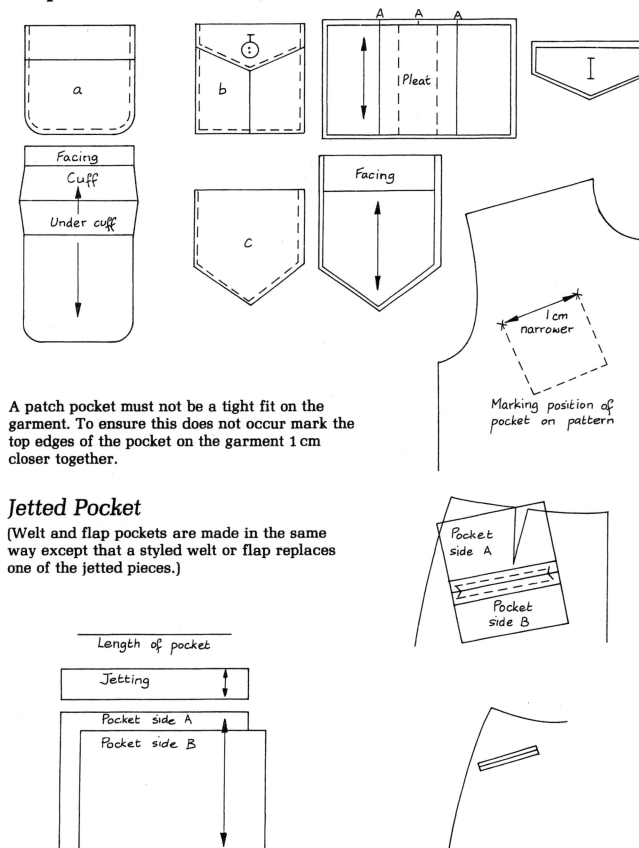

A patch pocket must not be a tight fit on the garment. To ensure this does not occur mark the top edges of the pocket on the garment 1 cm closer together.

Jetted Pocket

(Welt and flap pockets are made in the same way except that a styled welt or flap replaces one of the jetted pieces.)

More pockets are shown on page 87.

Halter Top

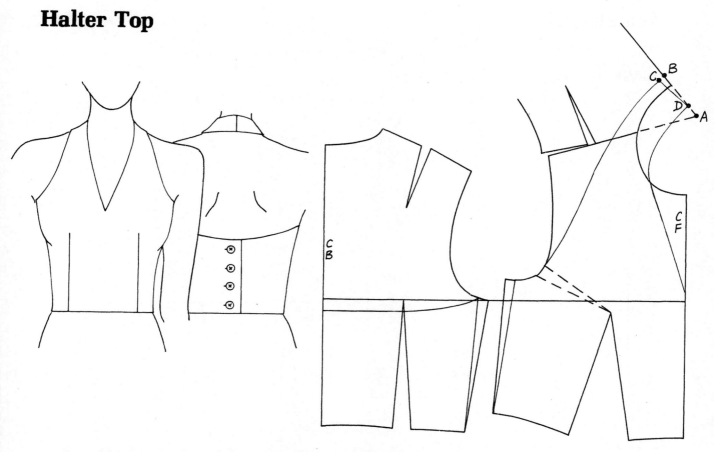

1. Line up blocks on chest line, swinging front shoulder dart into waist dart.
2. To avoid gaping at front arm hole, remove 2 cm into a temporary dart at the base of the arm hole.
3. Remove 1.5 cm tolerance from front and back side seams at arm hole. Draw in the lower back section.
4. Place shoulder line of back bodice block on to front. Continue front shoulder line and CB until they meet at A. A–B = 7 cm; B–C = 1 cm. Join C to A. A–D = 2 cm.
5. From 90° angles at C and D draw in strap lines, running into front bodice and through to CB. The front neck line is lowered by approx. 14 cm.
6. Trace off each section and combine into one pattern piece with one front waist dart which is shortened by 2 cm. Add allowance for fastening.

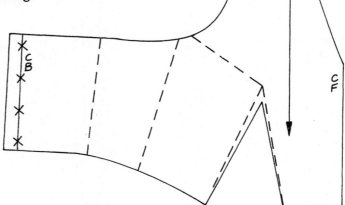

Waistcoats

Style 1   Fitted Waistcoat

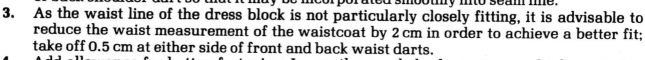

1. Line up dress blocks on chest line.
2. Draw in shaped hem line and divide front and back into four panels. It may be necessary to reposition base of back shoulder dart so that it may be incorporated smoothly into seam line.
3. As the waist line of the dress block is not particularly closely fitting, it is advisable to reduce the waist measurement of the waistcoat by 2 cm in order to achieve a better fit; take off 0.5 cm at either side of front and back waist darts.
4. Add allowance for button fastening. Lower the arm holes by 1–2 cm and take a similar amount from neck line and shoulder.

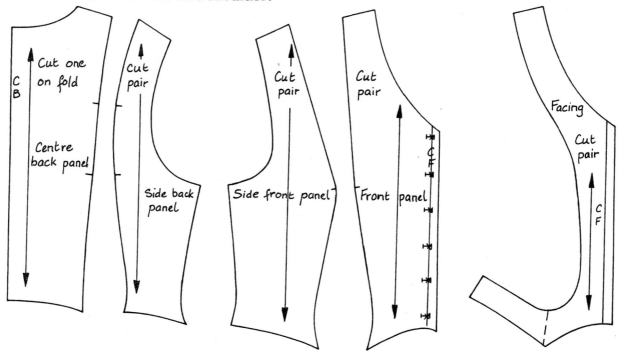

Style 2 Basic Box Waistcoat

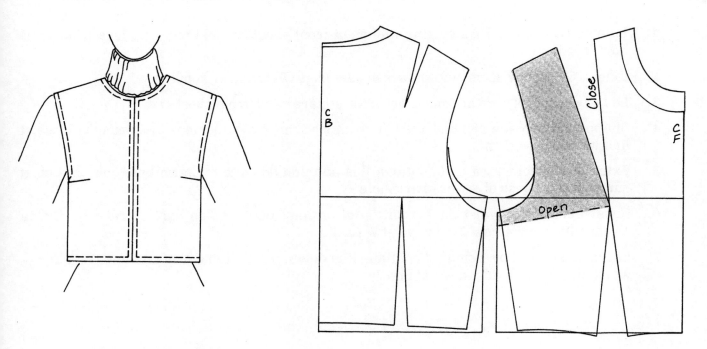

1. Line up bodice blocks on chest line.
2. Square across from waist point on CF across to CB.
3. Square down from chest line to new waist line and lower arm holes by 1 – 2 cm.
4. Swing front shoulder dart into new side seam and shorten by 2 cm.
5. Lower CF neck line 2 – 3 cm and widen it at the shoulder by 1 – 2 cm. Lower CB neck line 2 cm and widen it at the shoulder to match front alteration.

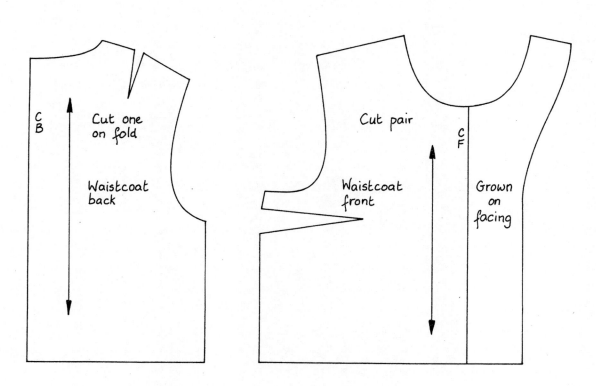

Basic Shirt Block

1. Line up bodice blocks, swinging volume of front shoulder dart into arm hole where it is now forgotten.

2. Extend CB line by 20 cm and square across from CB to CF for hemline.

3. Lower arm holes 1 cm and move out 1 cm; square down from chest line.

4. Shape in 2.5 cm at waist line and join to under arm points and hem line. Smooth off waist line with a curved line.

5. Extend shoulders 1 cm and continue this addition down to mid-arm hole. Join in a good curved line to base of lowered arm hole.

6. Construct a back waist dart from top of original back bodice dart, parallel to CB, to 14 cm below waist line; 2 cm wide at waist line.

7. Lower bust point by 2 cm and continue line down, parallel to CF, to a point 10 cm below waist line; 2.5 cm wide at waist line.

Basic Shirt Block

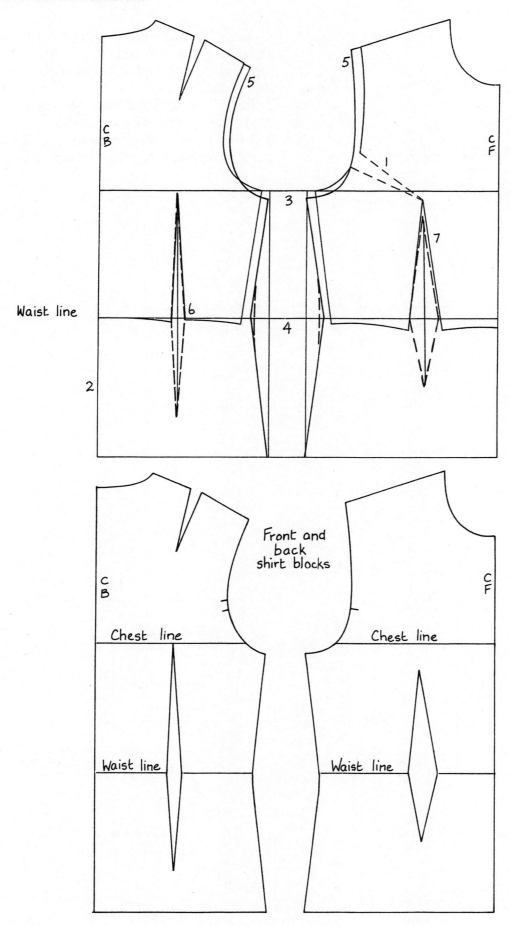

C B

C F

5

5

1

3

7

Waist line

6

2

4

Front and
back
shirt blocks

C B

C F

Chest line

Chest line

Waist line

Waist line

Basic Shirt Sleeve Block

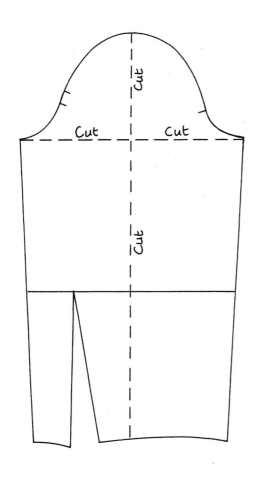

1. Outline the basic sleeve block. Cut along the under arm line and central line.
2. Open up 2 cm at the under arm level and wrist level.
3. Collapse crown until top edges meet.
4. Add 1 cm at the under arm level.
5. Mark in a new set of notches matching the basic shirt block. Mark in shoulder notch.

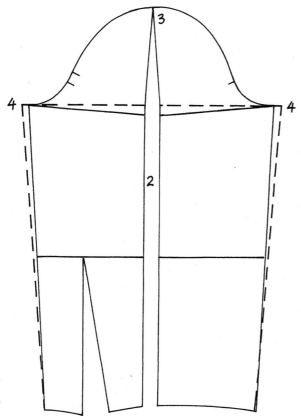

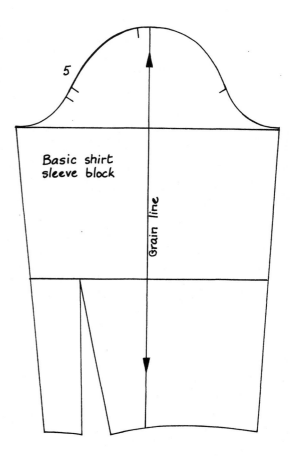

Basic shirt sleeve block

Grain line

Dress Block

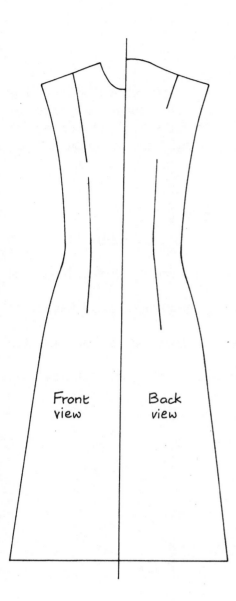

Front view · Back view

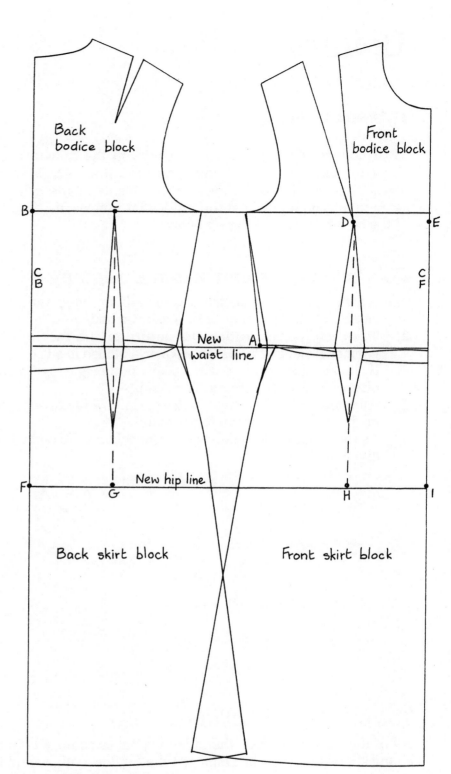

1. Line up bodice blocks on chest line. Extend CF and CB lines downwards and add skirt blocks (side points of waist touching only). Mark top points of bodice waist darts only—the remainder of dart markings are not required.
2. Mark in new waist line 1.5 cm down CB from bodice waist. Square across to CF. Mark in new hip line 20 cm below new waist line.
3. Smooth off side seams, taking 1 cm off front side seam at A.
4. Construct new darts: F–G = B–C, H–I = D–E. Join D to H for centre guide line for front dart. Shorten by 10 cm from H, and draw in dart, making the widest point 4 cm at waist line. Join C to G for centre guide line for back dart. Shorten by 8 cm from G, and draw in dart, making the widest point 2.5 cm at waist line.

Collars

Introduction

Most collars form two sections when on the human body or the stand. Although flat in construction, when attached to the neck line of a garment the collar forms two separate areas. The 'stand' is the area on the inside of the collar, next to the neck, from the neck seam to the roll line whilst the 'fall' is the outer area between the roll line and the outer edge of the collar (see left diagram below).

Points to remember when Designing a Collar

1. As the collar on a garment is usually an important focal point, it should be designed in relation to the garment it is to be attached to.
2. Take into consideration the nature of the fabric to be used and with which type of garment – i.e. is it a coat in wool or a blouse in silk?
3. If the garment is to be worn over another piece of clothing, the neck line will have to be altered before the collar is drafted.
4. All collars should be tested in toile before being accepted as correct, and some can often be modelled directly on to the stand.
5. As the outer edge is shortened, the collar will roll higher and closer to the neck (see right diagram below).

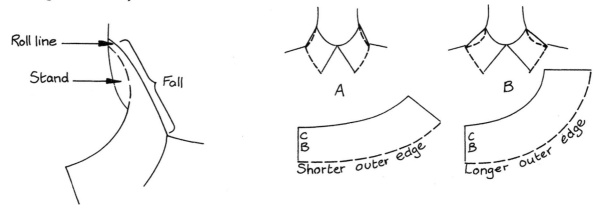

Top and Under Collars

All of the collar styles on the following pages require both a top and under collar. The basic collar shapes on the diagrams are the 'under' collars and we use these as the basis for the 'upper' collar shapes. An average of 0.3 cm is added to the outer edge of the collar, returning to the basic under collar shape at neck edge and any corners of the collar (see diagram below). This ensures that the seam at the outer edge is hidden when the collar is attached.

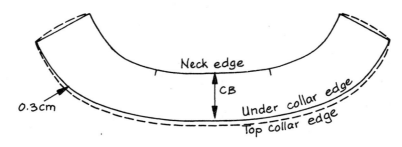

Part One – Basic Collars

Basic Peter Pan Collar

1. Lower neck 1 cm at CF.
2. Placing back and front neck points together, overlap around 4 cm at shoulder/arm hole points.
3. Draw in collar outline, approx. 6 cm deep. Angle where collar edge meets CB must be 90°.
4. Construct top collar from this under collar outline.

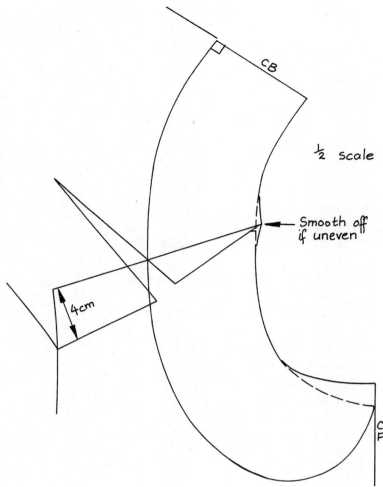

½ scale

Smooth off if uneven

4 cm

CB

CF

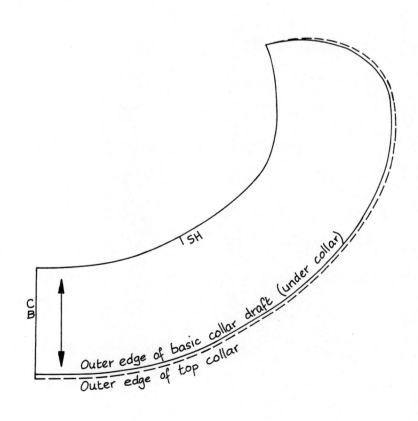

SH

C B

Outer edge of basic collar draft (under collar)

Outer edge of top collar

Roll Peter Pan Collar

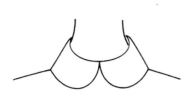

1. Lower neck 1 cm at CF.
2. Placing back and front neck points together, overlap around 7 cm at shoulder/arm hole points.
3. Draw in collar outline, approx. 6–8 cm deep. Angle where collar edge meets CB must be 90°.
4. Trace off collar shape and cut along the dotted lines; keep neck edges together whilst overlapping at outside edge 0.7 cm at both points.
5. Construct top collar from this under collar outline.

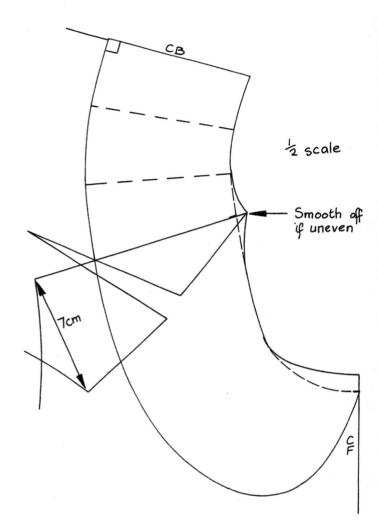

½ scale

Smooth off if uneven

7cm

CB

C F

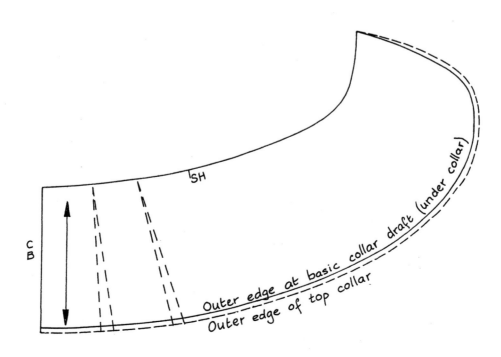

SH

C B

Outer edge at basic collar draft (under collar)

Outer edge of top collar

One-piece Shirt Collar

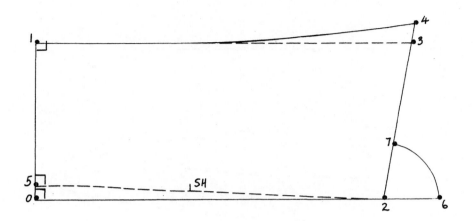

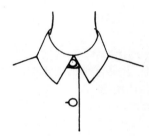

0–1 = collar depth of approx. 9 cm.

0–2 = $\frac{1}{2}$ neck line measurement.

1–3 = 0–2 plus 2 cm.

Join 2–3 and continue line 1 cm to 4.

Draw a smooth line down from 4 to line 1–3.

0–5 = 1 cm.

From a 90° angle at 5, draw a smooth line to 2.

2–6 = width of button wrap on garment.

2–7 = stand (2–3 cm).

Mark in shoulder notch.

Construct top collar from this under collar
    outline.

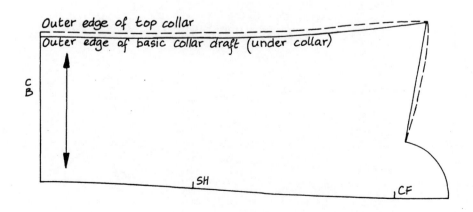

Two-piece Shirt Collar

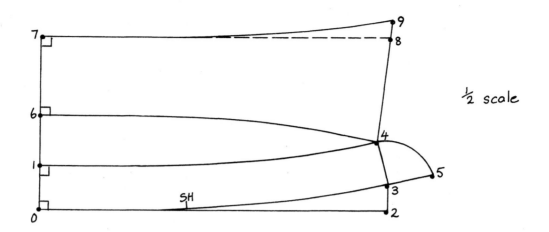

½ scale

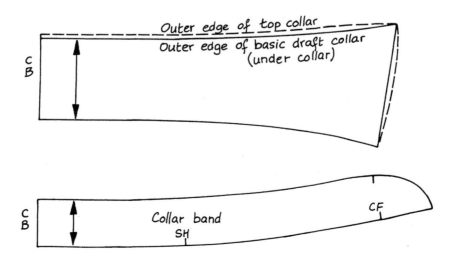

0–1 = 2.5 cm stand.

0–2 = ½ neck line measurement.

2–3 = 1.5 cm band shaping.

Draw a smooth line from 3 down to line 0–2.

3–4 = 2.5 cm stand. Draw a smooth line from 4 to 1, forming a stand of 2.5 cm depth.

3–5 = width of button wrap on garment.

0–6 = 5.5 cm. Join 6 to 4 in a smooth line of identical shape to corresponding line 1–4.

6–7 = 4.5 cm fall.

7–8 = 0–2.

8–9 = 1 cm. Draw in a smooth line from 9 down to line 7–8.

Mark in shoulder notch.

Construct top collar from the under collar outline (top part of collar only).

Stand Collar

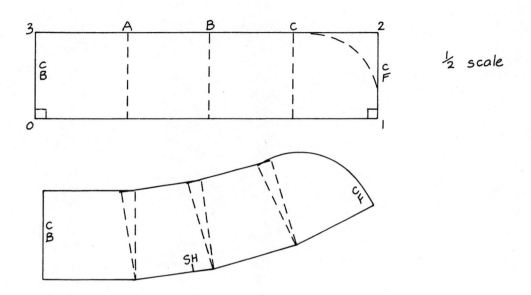

½ scale

$0-1 = \frac{1}{2}$ neck line measurement.

$\left.\begin{matrix} 1-2 \\ 0-3 \end{matrix}\right\}$ = height of collar.

Shape into curve at CF if required.

Slash collar at A, B and C, and reduce collar edge by a total of 2 cm on the $\frac{1}{2}$ pattern, keeping neck edge the original measurement.

Construct top collar from this under collar outline.

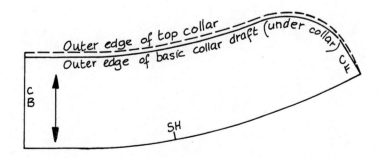

Sailor Collar

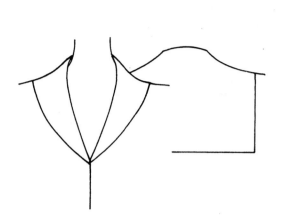

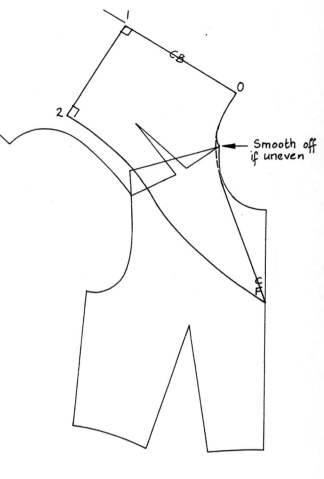

Smooth off if uneven

1. Lower front neck line as required.
2. Placing front and back neck points together overlap shoulder/arm hole points by approx. 4–7 cm depending on the roll required.
3. Draw in collar outline: 0–1 = 15–20 cm. Square across from 1 to 2.
4. Construct top collar from this under collar outline as shown below.

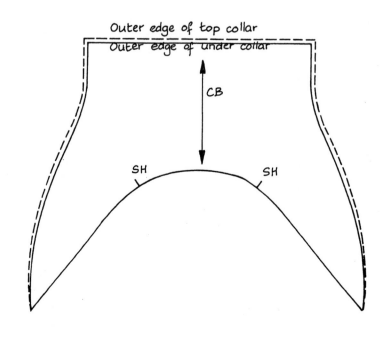

Outer edge of top collar
Outer edge of under collar

Grown-on Collar

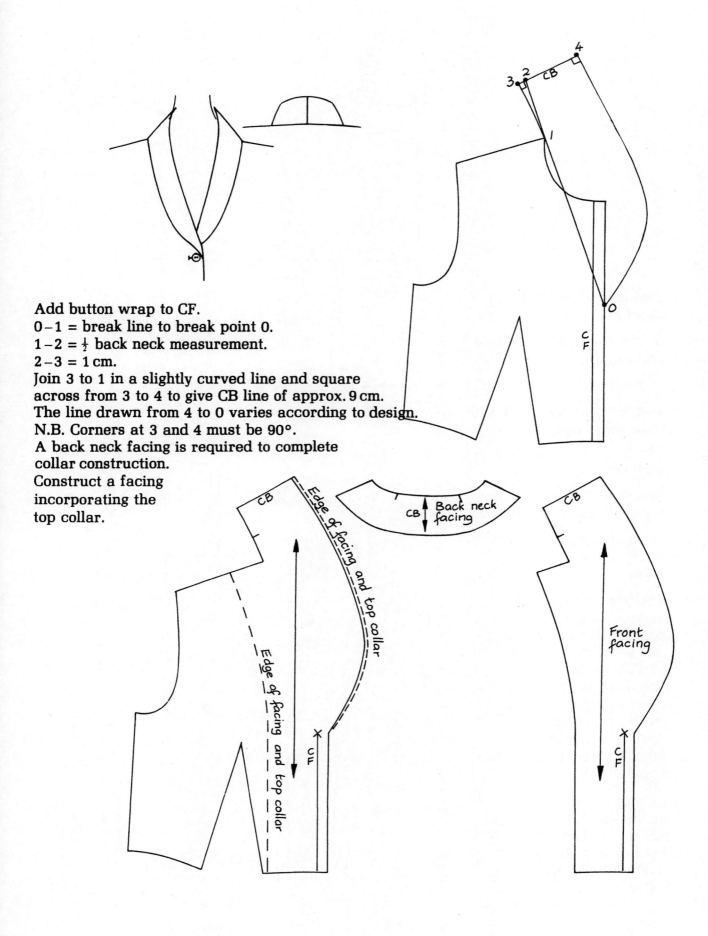

Add button wrap to CF.

0–1 = break line to break point 0.

1–2 = ½ back neck measurement.

2–3 = 1 cm.

Join 3 to 1 in a slightly curved line and square
across from 3 to 4 to give CB line of approx. 9 cm.

The line drawn from 4 to 0 varies according to design.

N.B. Corners at 3 and 4 must be 90°.

A back neck facing is required to complete
collar construction.

Construct a facing
incorporating the
top collar.

High Neck Line with Flyaway Collar

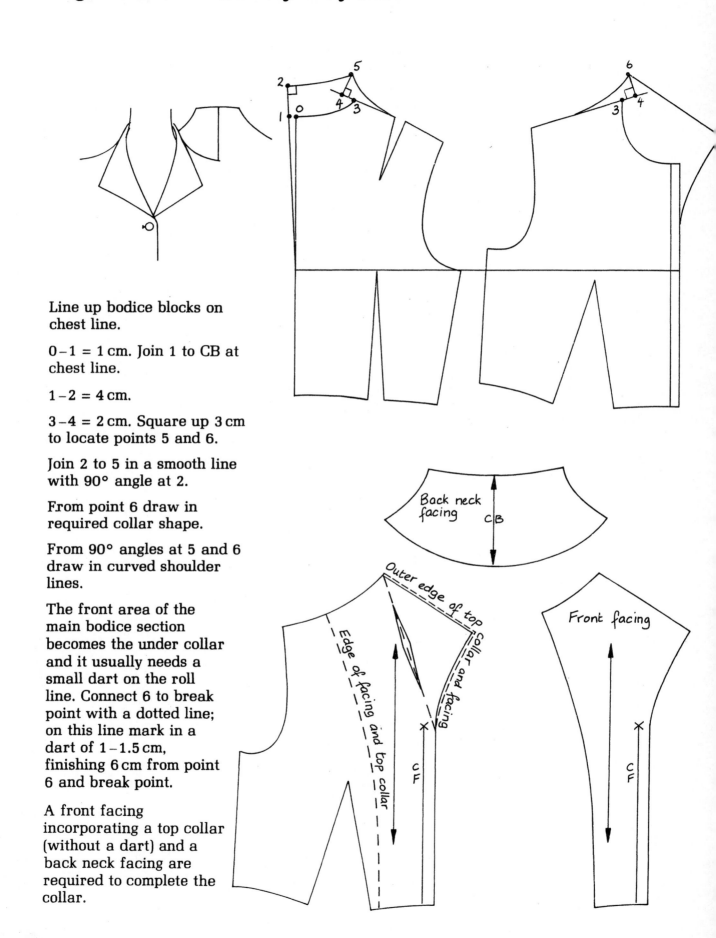

Line up bodice blocks on chest line.

0–1 = 1 cm. Join 1 to CB at chest line.

1–2 = 4 cm.

3–4 = 2 cm. Square up 3 cm to locate points 5 and 6.

Join 2 to 5 in a smooth line with 90° angle at 2.

From point 6 draw in required collar shape.

From 90° angles at 5 and 6 draw in curved shoulder lines.

The front area of the main bodice section becomes the under collar and it usually needs a small dart on the roll line. Connect 6 to break point with a dotted line; on this line mark in a dart of 1–1.5 cm, finishing 6 cm from point 6 and break point.

A front facing incorporating a top collar (without a dart) and a back neck facing are required to complete the collar.

Part Two—Tailored Collars

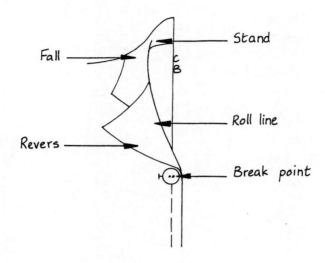

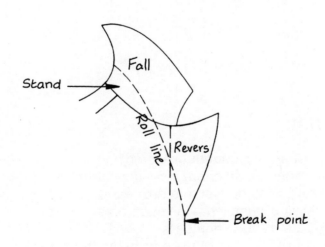

Basic Tailored Collar Draft

0–1 = 2.5 cm stand.

   2 = break point.

1–2 = roll line.

1–3 = ½ back neck measurement.

3–4 = 2.5 cm collar diversion

      *4 is then joined to 1, and 5 and 6
are at 90° (4 can alternatively
be joined to 1A).

4–5 = 2.5 cm stand.

4–6 = 5 cm fall.

      From a 90° angle at 5 and 6
design your collar shape.

N.B. The shaded area at 0
belongs to both the
upper collar and the shoulder
of the garment.

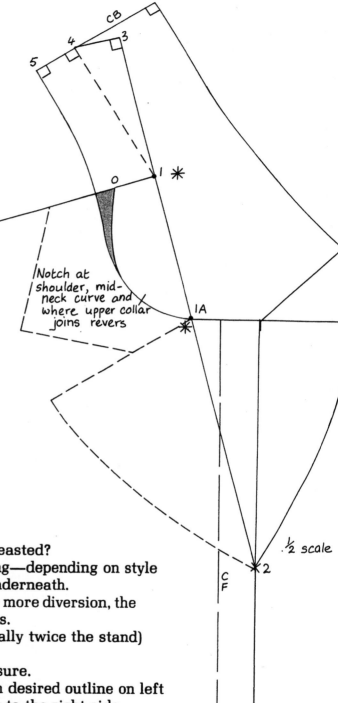

Notch at shoulder, mid-neck curve and where upper collar joins revers

½ scale

Points to remember

1. Size of button wrap; single or double breasted?
2. Whether size of neck line needs changing—depending on style
   and whether a garment is to be worn underneath.
3. Amount of collar diversion required—the more diversion, the
   flatter the collar will lie on the shoulders.
4. Amount of stand and fall (the fall is usually twice the stand)
   and position of roll line.
5. Position of break point—the point of closure.
6. Shape of revers and upper collar: sketch desired outline on left
   side of break line first and then transfer to the right side.

Collar Diversion

Method 1

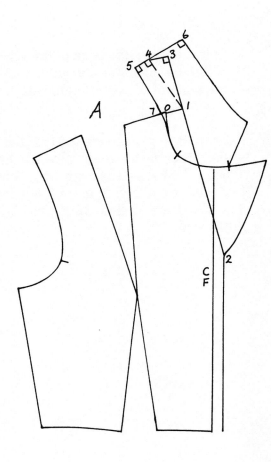

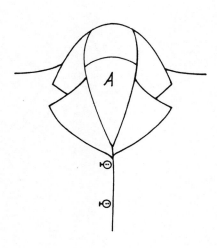

Basic draft A has 2.5 cm diversion which gives a fairly high, close fitting collar. Draft B shows a lower lying collar—this is obtained by diverting 5 cm which gives a collar with a longer outside edge, enabling it to lie further onto the shoulders. Check that 5–7 is the same measurement as 5–7 on draft A. The diversion could be as much as 7 cm which gives a very flat upper collar.

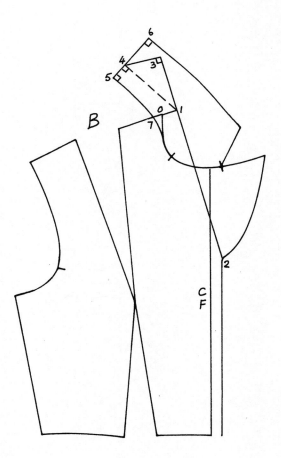

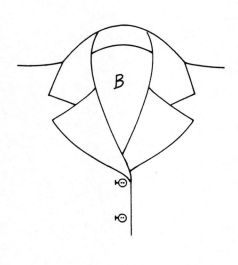

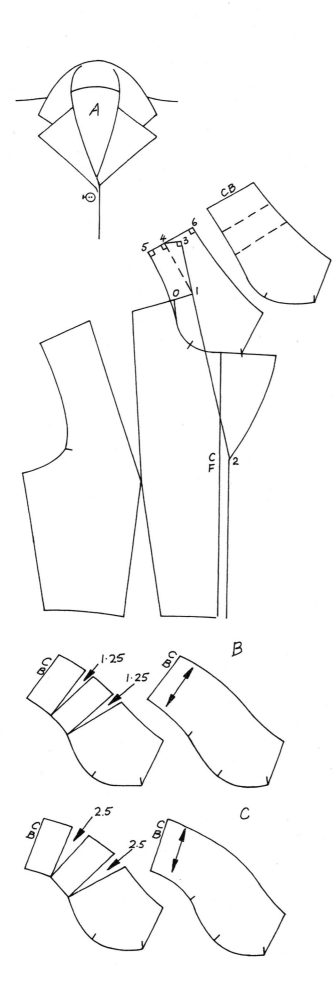

Method 2

Enlarge the outer edge of the upper collar by slashing and introducing the amount of diversion necessary.

Draft B has an extra 2.5 cm diversion (the basic shape already has been diverted 2.5 cm in construction) allowed in outer edge, while draft C has an extra 5 cm allowed.

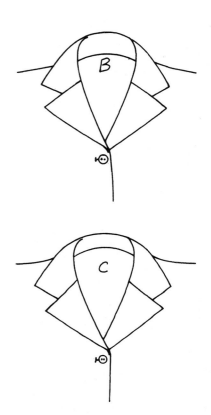

Tailored Collar Styles

1. *Double Breasted Collar with Set-away Neck*

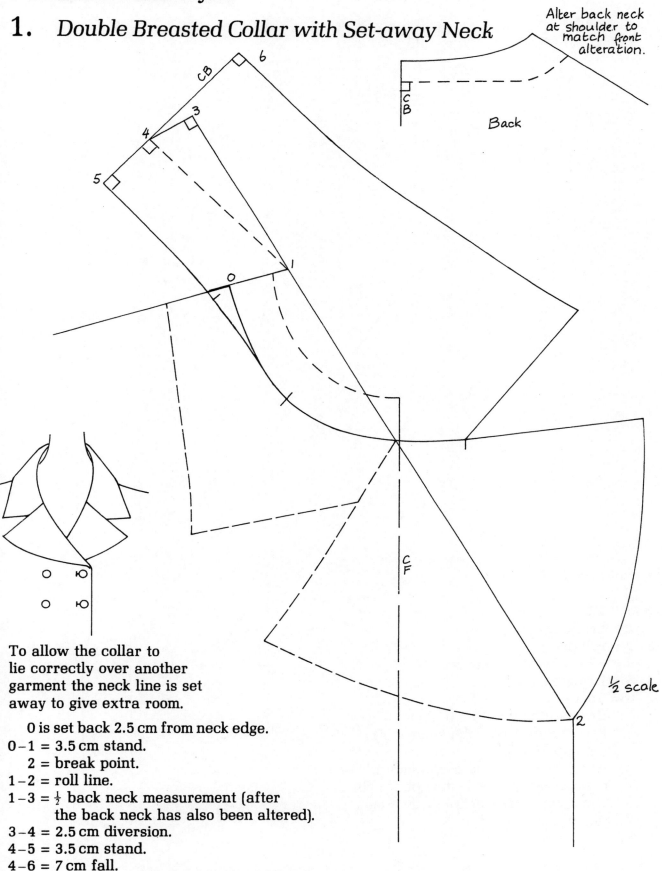

Alter back neck at shoulder to match front alteration.

Back

To allow the collar to lie correctly over another garment the neck line is set away to give extra room.

    0 is set back 2.5 cm from neck edge.
0–1 = 3.5 cm stand.
    2 = break point.
1–2 = roll line.
1–3 = $\frac{1}{2}$ back neck measurement (after
       the back neck has also been altered).
3–4 = 2.5 cm diversion.
4–5 = 3.5 cm stand.
4–6 = 7 cm fall.
      From 90° at 6 and 5 draw collar shape.

$\frac{1}{2}$ scale

2. Low Revers and Squared Neck

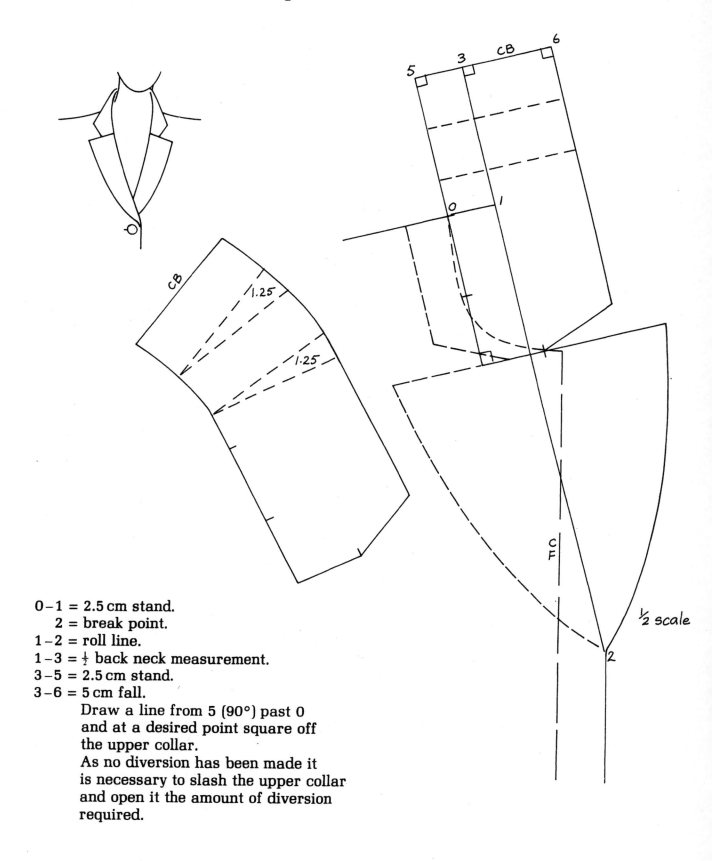

0–1 = 2.5 cm stand.

   2 = break point.

1–2 = roll line.

1–3 = $\frac{1}{2}$ back neck measurement.

3–5 = 2.5 cm stand.

3–6 = 5 cm fall.

   Draw a line from 5 (90°) past 0
and at a desired point square off
the upper collar.

   As no diversion has been made it
is necessary to slash the upper collar
and open it the amount of diversion
required.

3. *Collar with Curved Revers*

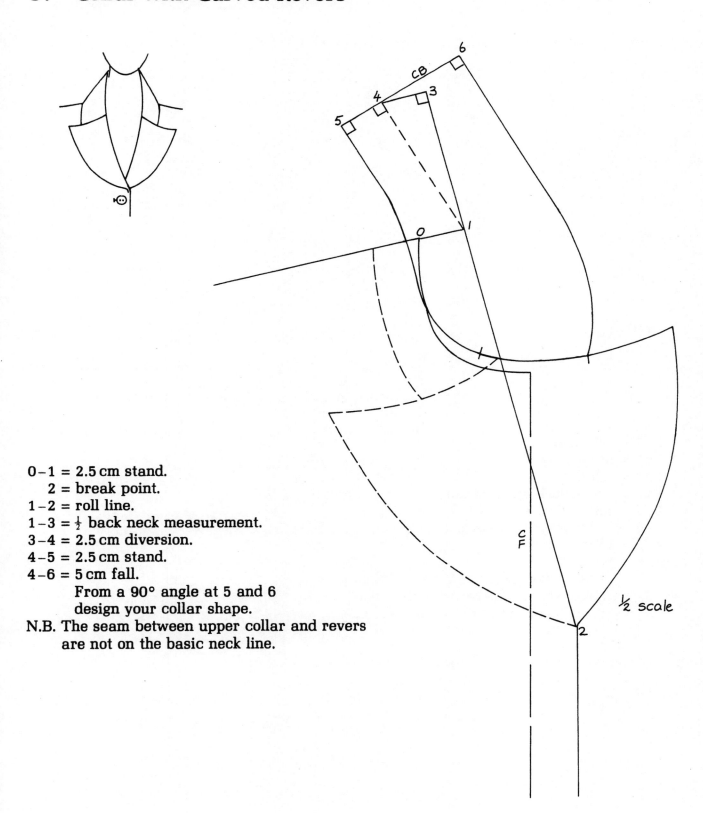

0–1 = 2.5 cm stand.

   2 = break point.

1–2 = roll line.

1–3 = $\frac{1}{2}$ back neck measurement.

3–4 = 2.5 cm diversion.

4–5 = 2.5 cm stand.

4–6 = 5 cm fall.

     From a 90° angle at 5 and 6
     design your collar shape.

N.B. The seam between upper collar and revers
     are not on the basic neck line.

4. Collar with Pointed Revers

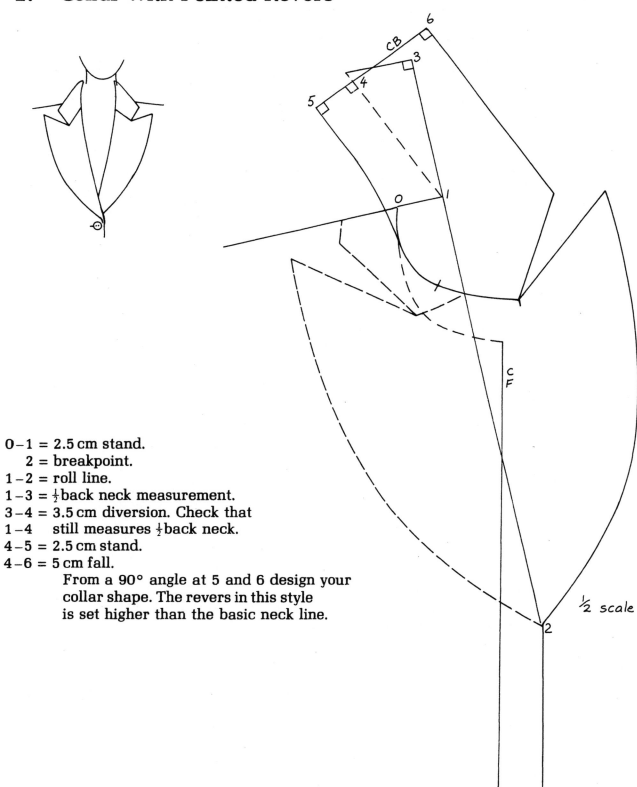

0-1 = 2.5 cm stand.
  2 = breakpoint.
1-2 = roll line.
1-3 = $\frac{1}{2}$ back neck measurement.
3-4 = 3.5 cm diversion. Check that
1-4   still measures $\frac{1}{2}$ back neck.
4-5 = 2.5 cm stand.
4-6 = 5 cm fall.
      From a 90° angle at 5 and 6 design your
      collar shape. The revers in this style
      is set higher than the basic neck line.

Facings for Tailored Collars

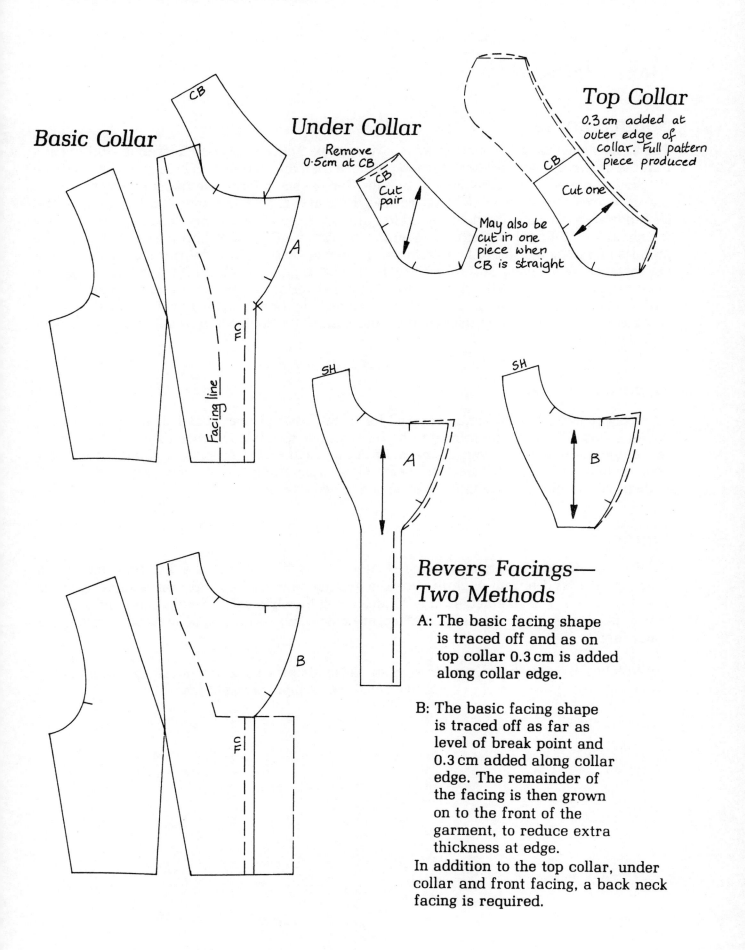

Basic Collar

CB

Facing line

CF

Under Collar

Remove 0·5cm at CB

CB

Cut pair

May also be cut in one piece when CB is straight

Top Collar

0.3 cm added at outer edge of collar. Full pattern piece produced

CB

Cut one

A

SH

A

B

SH

B

CF

Revers Facings— Two Methods

A: The basic facing shape is traced off and as on top collar 0.3 cm is added along collar edge.

B: The basic facing shape is traced off as far as level of break point and 0.3 cm added along collar edge. The remainder of the facing is then grown on to the front of the garment, to reduce extra thickness at edge.

In addition to the top collar, under collar and front facing, a back neck facing is required.

Sleeves

Sleeve Patterns

Set-in Sleeves

The basic sleeve block is constructed to give approx. 2 cm sleeve head tolerance—this means that the crown of the sleeve measures 2 cm more than the area of arm hole to which it is to be stitched. We need this extra amount to allow for the shoulder. If we had no tolerance at all the crown of the sleeve would be rather tight and restricting over the upper arm and shoulder area, so the more sleeve head tolerance we can afford to use, the better the fit over the shoulder. We ease this extra amount of fabric into the upper half of the arm hole. The process of easing the sleeve head tolerance is easier with certain fabrics than with others. For instance, when using soft fabrics such as wool or jersey we can afford to have a surplus of up to 6 cm to ease into the arm hole whilst with fabrics like silk or cotton we would find it difficult to ease more than 2–2.5 cm into the arm hole. Before using any new blocks always check what the sleeve head tolerance is, and mark it on the block in readiness for use with different fabrics.

Raglan Sleeves

All of the sleeve head tolerance allowed for in the basic sleeve block is lost when creating raglan styles. We have, therefore, to be particularly careful when we draw in the curved dart at the shoulder of the raglan sleeve. Do not make this dart too long—it should preferably have smooth, curved and relatively short sides. Raglan styles are most successful when made in soft, pliable fabrics that 'give' when the arms are in movement.

Kimonos

As with raglans, kimono styles are more suited to soft fabrics but for a different reason. All kimono styles tend to pull slightly over the shoulder area when the arm is hanging in its natural position. The strained area is relieved slightly when soft fabric is used and also the folds of fabric created underneath the arm are not so bulky as when the garment is made in a firmer fabric.

N.B. Notches are extremely important in any form of pattern making but sleeves of all types **must** have all required notches marked on each pattern piece and block.

Basic Sleeve Block

Measurements—Size 12
Under arm length = 43 cm.
Wrist = 15.4 cm.
Scale as bodice draft = 39 cm.

Code
0–1 = under arm length.
2 = midway 0–1.
0–3 = 3–4 on bodice draft.
Square across from 0, 1, 2 and 3.
0–4 = ½ scye measurement (measure arm hole on bodice draft).
0–8 = 3–4.
5 = midway 3–4.
Square down to 6.
5–7 = $\frac{1}{10}$ scale, less 2 cm (this gives approx. 2 cm sleeve head tolerance).
$\left.\begin{array}{c} 0–9 \\ 8–10 \end{array}\right\}$ = 10–9 and 10–8 on bodice draft + 1 cm on either side.
$\left.\begin{array}{c} 6–11 \\ 6–12 \end{array}\right\}$ = ½ wrist measurement + 2 cm dart allowance + 3 cm ease.
13–14 = 2 cm.
14–15 = 4 cm dart allowance.
Square up from 14 to locate 16.
Join 15 to 16.
17–16 = 15–16.

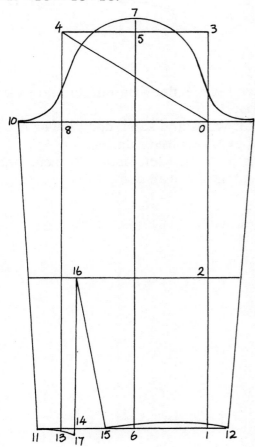

Completing Draft

1. Fold out wrist dart and connect 11 to 12, raising curve slightly between 15 and 12.
2. To form sleeve head connect 10 to 7 and 7 to 9, missing points 3 and 4 by approx. 2.5 cm. Use the lower arm hole shaping of bodice to determine correct curves and notches.

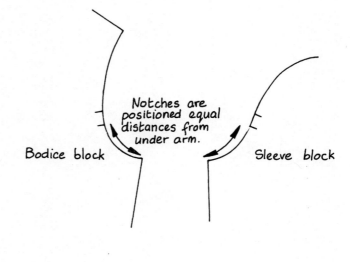

Notches are positioned equal distances from under arm.

Bodice block   Sleeve block

Set-in Sleeve Styles

1.

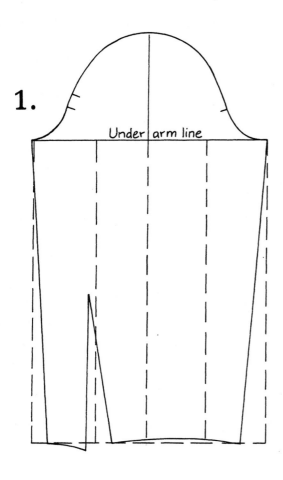

Under arm line

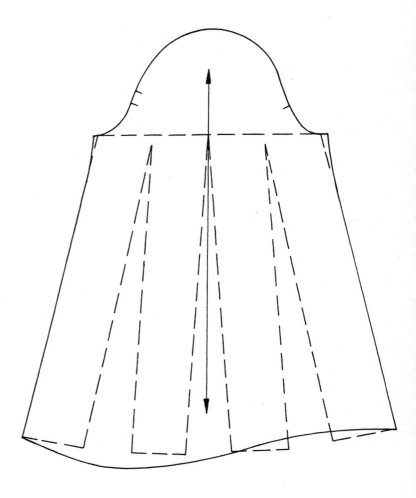

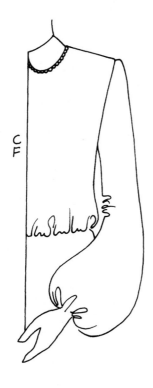

C
F

1. Square down from under arm line to add extra width at wrist.
2. Straighten off wrist and slash open lower area of sleeve to put in required fullness.
3. Lower back hem area of sleeve 2–3 cm and heighten front the same amount.

2.

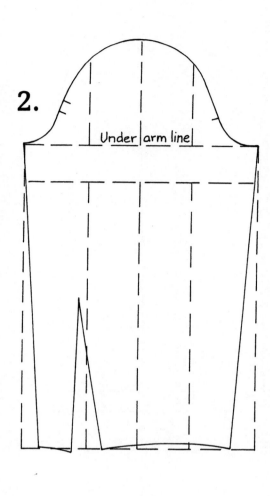

Under arm line

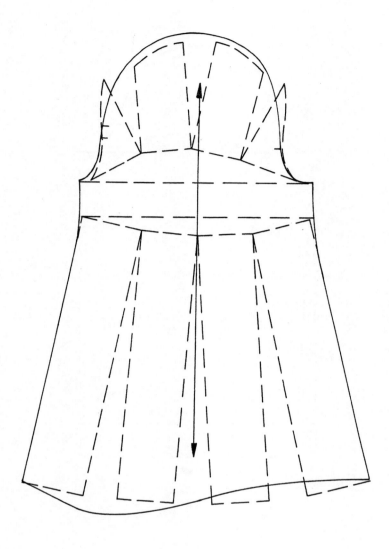

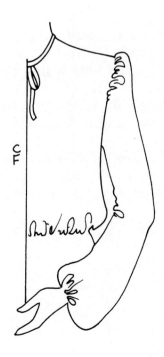

CF

1. Square down from under arm line to add extra width at wrist.
2. Straighten off wrist and slash open lower area of sleeve and crown area to put in fullness required.
3. Lower back hem area of sleeve 2–3 cm and heighten front the same amount.

3.

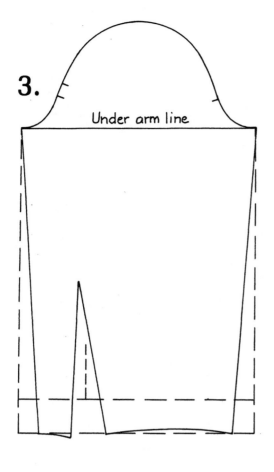

Under arm line

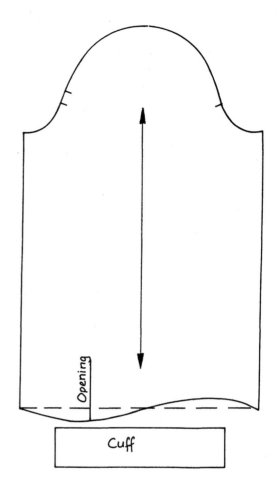

Opening

Cuff

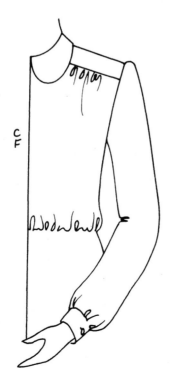

C
F

1. Square down from under arm line to add extra width at wrist.
2. Straighten off wrist with a line parallel to under arm line.
3. Decide on depth of cuff to be attached to sleeve; shorten sleeve by 2 cm less than this cuff depth.
4. Mark opening line of 6–8 cm and lower back hem area of sleeve 1.5 cm and heighten the front the same amount.

4.

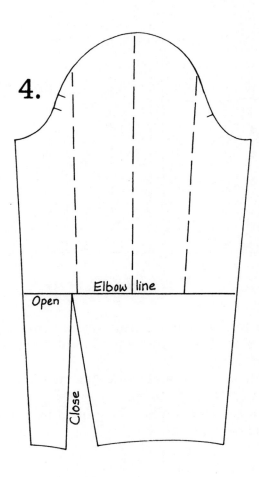

Open

Elbow line

Close

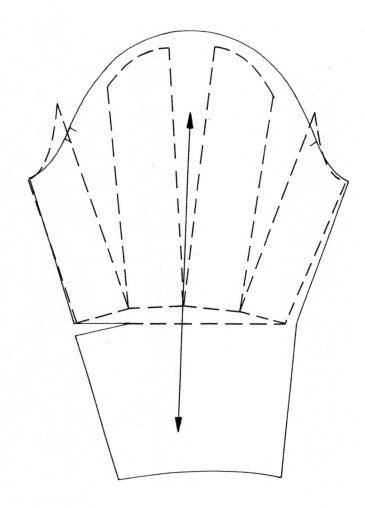

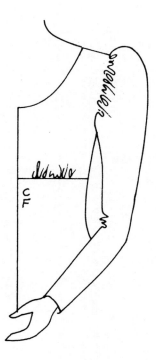

1. Slash open area above elbow line and open up crown the required amount.
2. Swing wrist to elbow dart into side seam.
3. Measure from under arm points to mark in arm hole notches.

5.

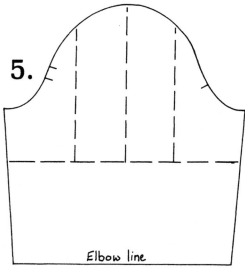

Elbow line

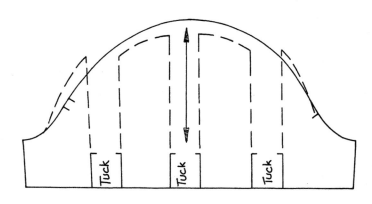

Tuck   Tuck   Tuck

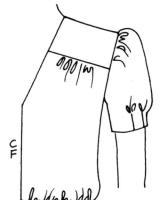

C F

1. Shorten sleeve required amount and slash open on three lines, equidistant from each other.
2. Open outwards and mark tuck positioning in 5 cm upwards from hem.
3. Measure from under arm points to position arm hole notches.

6.

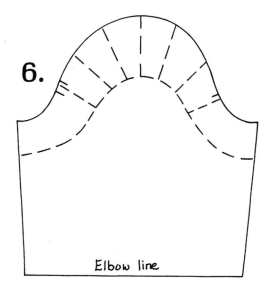

Elbow line

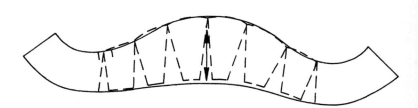

1. Draw out curved line as in diagram.
2. Slash open and, keeping crown points together, open outwards at hem.

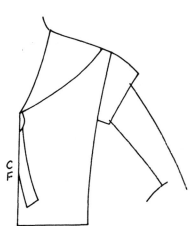

C F

7.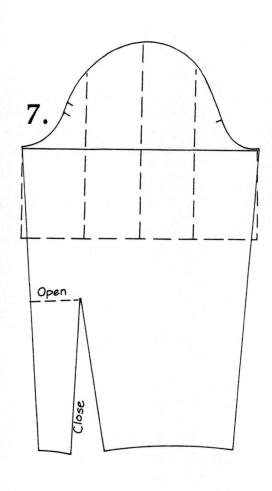

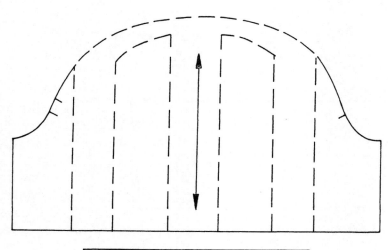

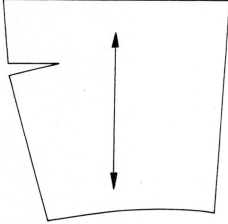

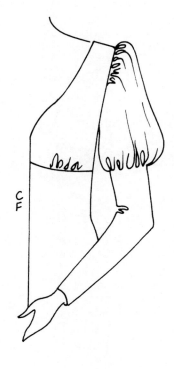

1. Square down from under arm line to depth required for top section of sleeve.
2. Open up to almost twice its original width.
3. Swing wrist dart into side seam at elbow level.

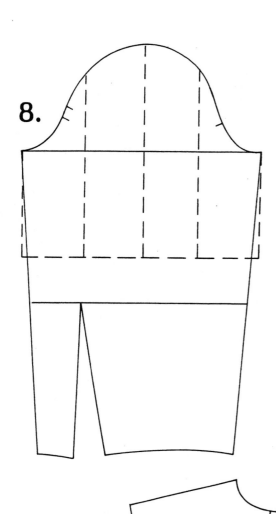

8.

1. Square down from under arm line to depth required for sleeve length.
2. Divide into four or more sections and open up at hem line, keeping top area of sleeve together.
3. Mark in the grain line at 45° to centre of sleeve and smooth off hem with an even curved line.

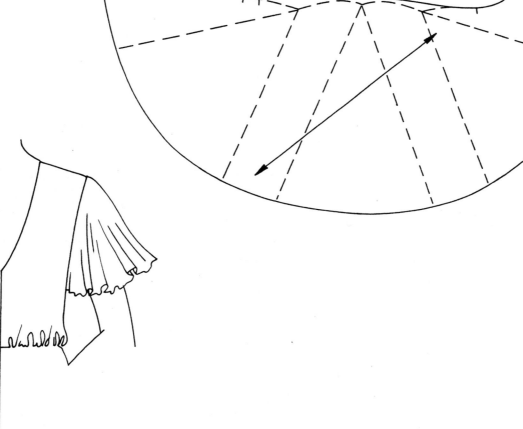

C
F

Sleeves with Padded Shoulders

1. Swing wrist dart into side seam at elbow level.
2. Draw in a smooth curve approx. 4–5 cm below crown of sleeve; position notches.
3. Open up shoulder section with crown area positioned on a straight line; smooth off lower edge.
4. Open up main part of sleeve keeping wrist edge together. Measure lower edge of shoulder section and make sure that the top edge of the main sleeve measures the same amount.

N.B. This style requires padding to support shoulder.

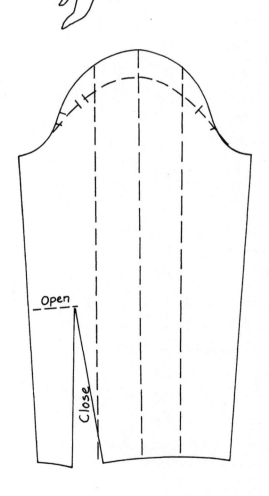

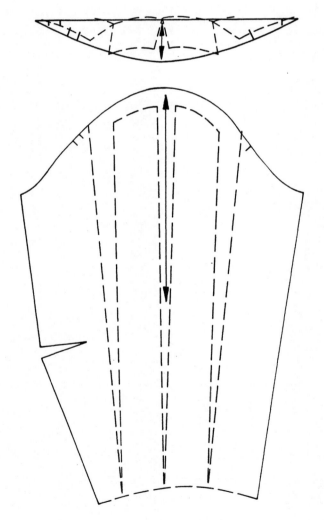

2.

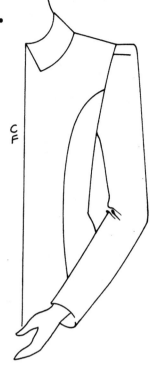

1. Divide up top area of sleeve and open up as in diagram.
2. Mark in three darts from crown in the direction of slash lines; approx. 3–4 cm in length.

N.B. This style requires padding to support shoulder.

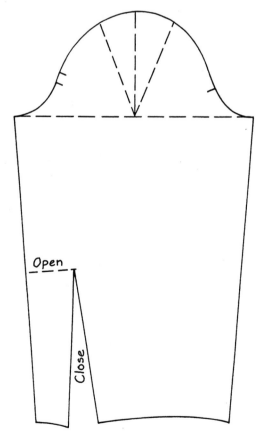

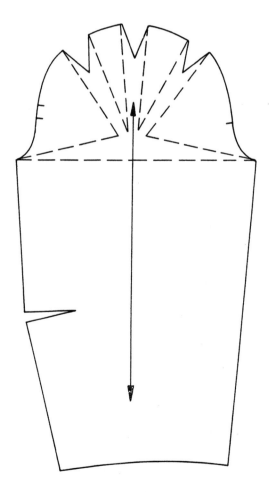

3.

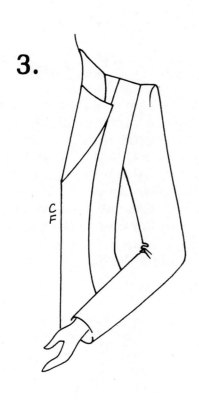

1. Follow instructions as for Style No. 2.
2. Trace off the two central sections of the crown, between the darts; close the outer darts by adding these two sections.
3. Smooth off any uneven areas on crown

N.B. This style requires padding to support shoulder.

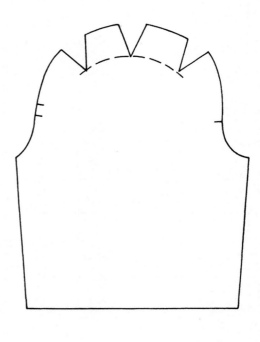

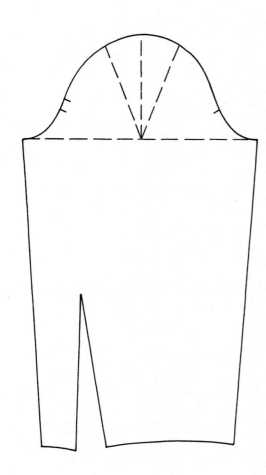

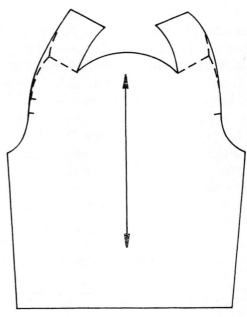

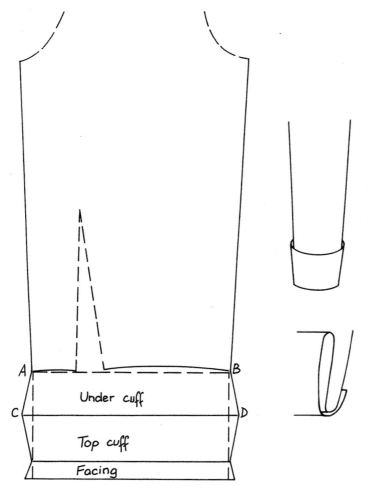

Cuffs

1. *Turn Back Cuff*

Straighten hem and square down from each corner. Mark double the width of cuff required and then add a facing. Make C to D at least 1 cm longer than A to B to allow cuff to lie smoothly over sleeve. If a closely fitting cuff is required move dart into elbow position first, making sure that the cuff is wide enough to accommodate the hand.

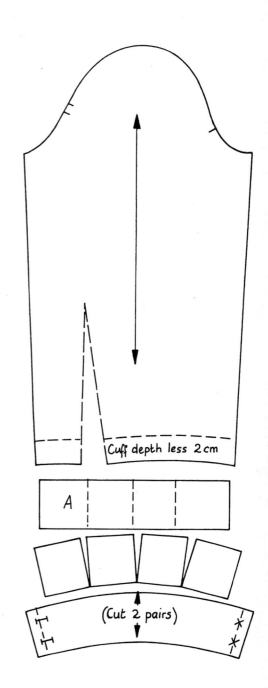

2. *Shirt Cuff*

Decide on depth of cuff and remove 2 cm less than this amount from the length of the sleeve. Draw a rectangle the depth of cuff by the wrist measurement + 2 cm (A). To this rectangle add an allowance for button hole and button extensions; double this shape to give full cuff (B). A cuff deeper than 5 cm needs to be shaped. After drawing the rectangle required slash and open to give a curved cuff; smooth off angles and add extensions.

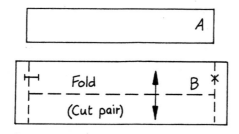

Raglan Sleeve Styles

1. *High Raglan*

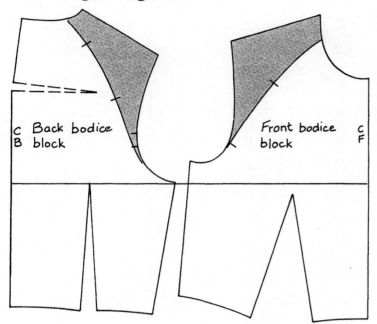

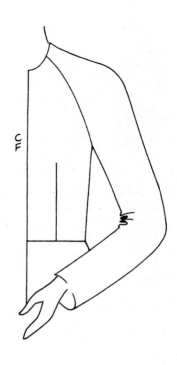

1. Line up bodice blocks and temporarily swing back shoulder dart into CB. Draw in raglan shape.
2. Trace off each shoulder section after notching raglan seam line.
3. Match arm hole notches and allow shoulder points of raglan to touch crown of sleeve.
4. Draw in a smooth curved dart over shoulder area from shoulder lines; no longer than 7 cm. Return back shoulder dart to original position where it is eased into the seam line.

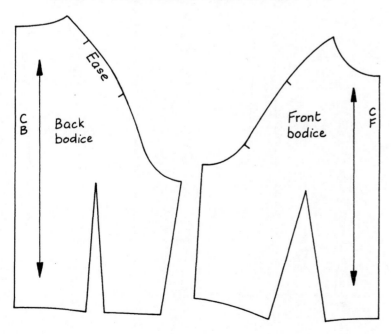

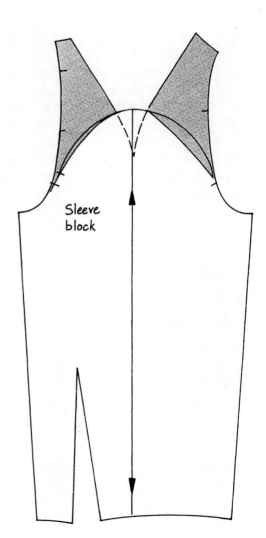

2. High Raglan with Yoke

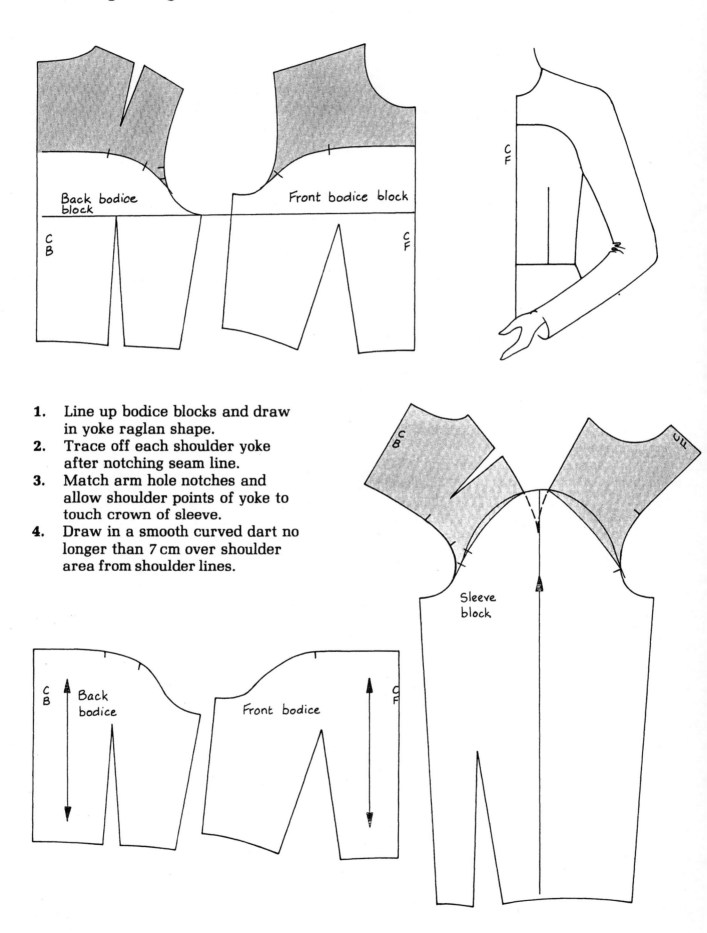

1. Line up bodice blocks and draw in yoke raglan shape.
2. Trace off each shoulder yoke after notching seam line.
3. Match arm hole notches and allow shoulder points of yoke to touch crown of sleeve.
4. Draw in a smooth curved dart no longer than 7 cm over shoulder area from shoulder lines.

Back bodice block

Front bodice block

C B

C F

Back bodice

Front bodice

Sleeve block

3. Deep Raglan

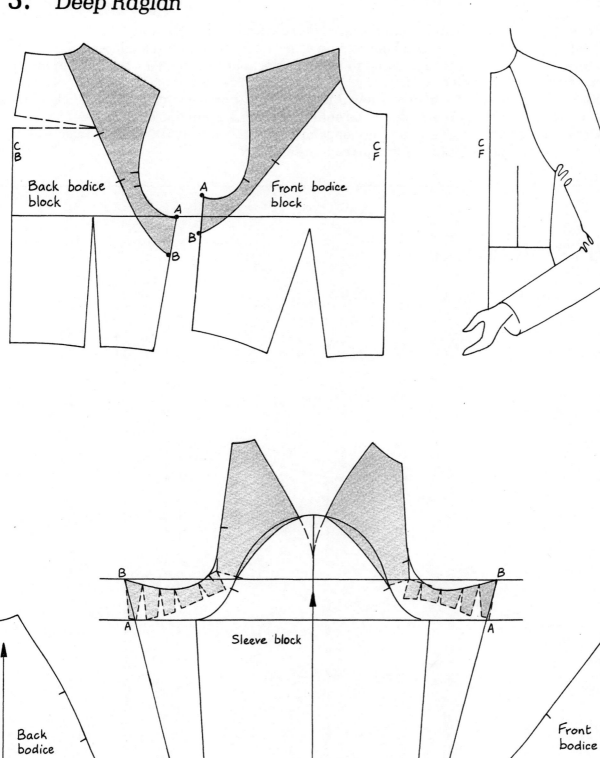

Deep Raglan continued

1. Line up bodice blocks and temporarily swing back shoulder dart into CB.
2. Trace off each shoulder/arm hole section after notching raglan seam lines.
3. Draw in a line above and parallel to the under arm line on sleeve—the amount dropped at under arm on bodice (A –B).
4. Slash in to base of arm hole to allow B to touch new line, when original arm hole notches are touching. Both points B should be equidistant from grain line of sleeve.
5. Draw in a smooth curved dart, no longer than 7 cm, over shoulder area from shoulder lines. Swing back shoulder dart into raglan seam line.

Basic Kimono Block

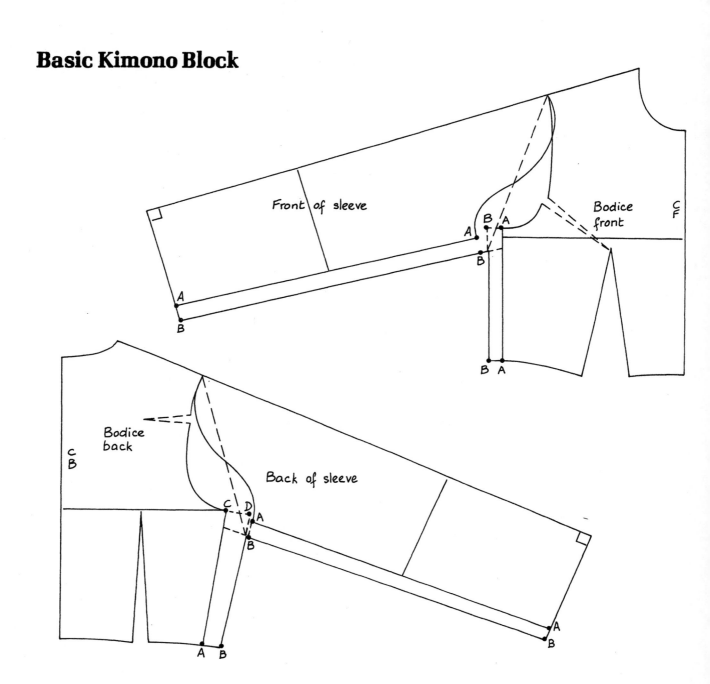

Kimono Block continued

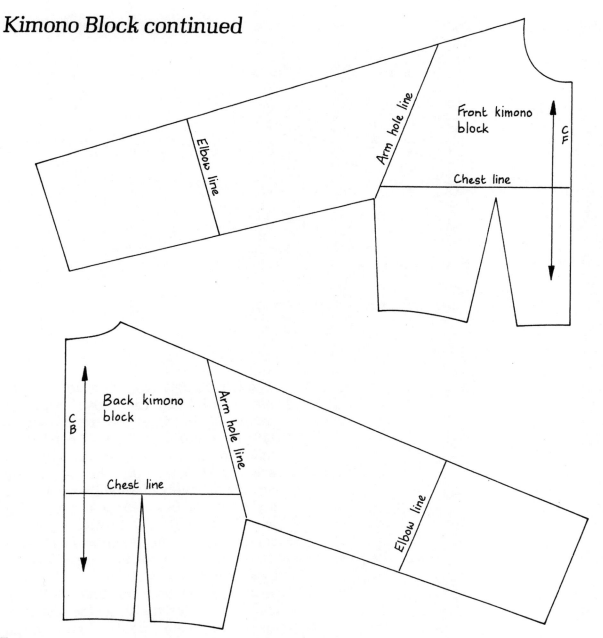

Front
1. Swing half volume of front shoulder dart into arm hole and the remainder into waist dart.
2. Continue shoulder line and place front half of sleeve on to this line; the crown must be touching the shoulder.
3. Straighten wrist by squaring across from base of new extended shoulder seam.
4. A–B = 2 cm. Mark in new arm hole guide line from shoulder to under arm point.

Back
1. Swing shoulder dart into arm hole.
2. Continue shoulder line and place back half of sleeve onto this line; the crown must be touching the shoulder.
3. Straighten wrist by squaring across from base of new extended shoulder seam.
4. A–B = 2 cm. C–D = 3 cm. Mark in new arm hole guide line from shoulder to under arm point.

N.B. Always check that the under arm length and the shoulder to wrist lines are the same length in both the back and the front blocks.

Angles of Kimonos

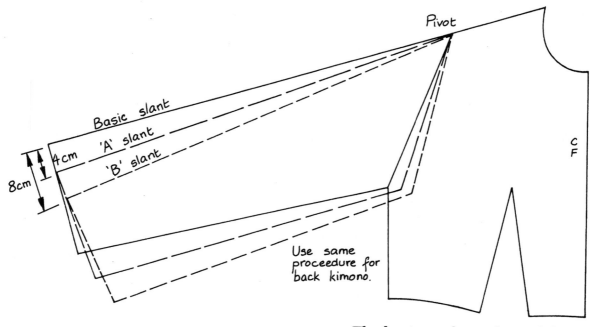

Basic slant
'A' slant
'B' slant
4 cm
8 cm
Pivot
C F

Use same proceedure for back kimono.

The basic angle or slant of the Kimono block allows the arm upward movement, but when the arm is lowered into its natural position, the garment tends to fit badly over the shoulder area. Soft fabric that has a certain amount of 'give' usually suits any kimono style but this basic shape in particular benefits from its use. By pivoting at the shoulder point we can alter the slant of the sleeve. 'A' slant has been lowered by 4 cm at the wrist, whilst 'B' slant has been lowered by 8 cm. The lower the slant the better the fit at the shoulder area and the tighter and more restricting is the under arm area. 'B' slant would therefore require a gusset to give more length to the under arm; 'A' slant also will need a gusset unless made in a stretchy, jersey-type fabric.

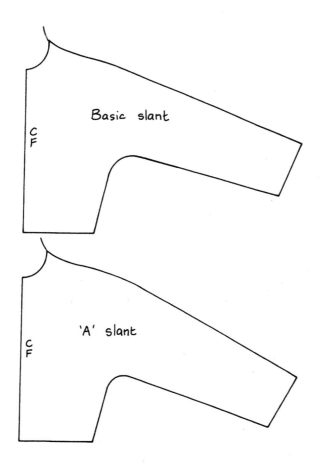

Basic slant
C F
'A' slant
C F

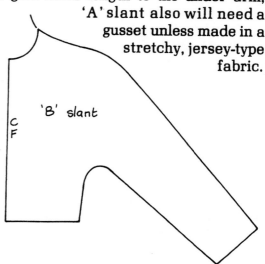

'B' slant
C F

Kimono Gussets

1. *Standard Gusset*

1. Mark in gusset line as it will have changed position (measure up from A along arm hole line 9 cm and towards CF and CB 2 cm), to B.

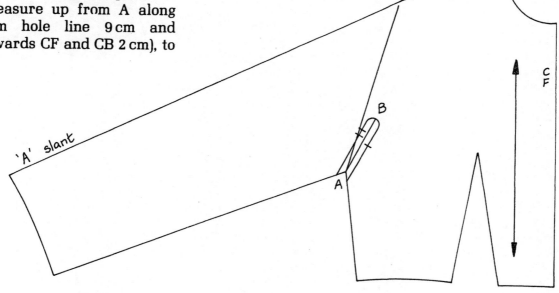

2. Mark in a line 1 cm around gusset line and notch at each side. This new line is the actual line of stitching and the gusset line is cut open to include a separate gusset.

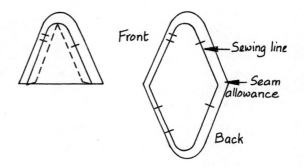

3. Trace off this gusset band and cut along centre line; open up to allow sufficient room for the under arm seam to return to its former length in basic block. Add seam allowance to this new gusset shape and cut on fold to give one piece for front and back. Notch the back section to match identical back gusset line.

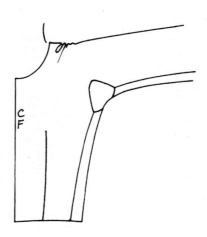

2. Strip Gusset

1. Draw in required strip panel and notch. Trace off and cut along gusset line.

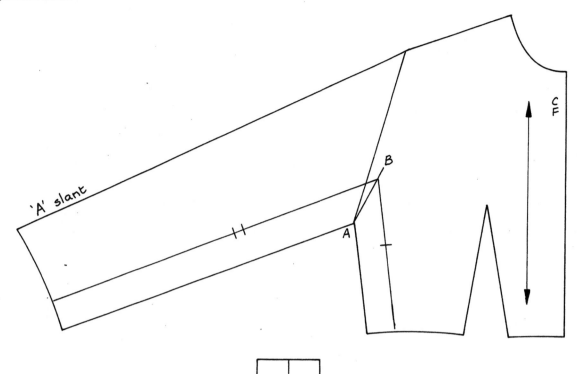

2. Place back and front strip panels together on to a central line to give one under arm panel.

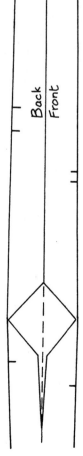

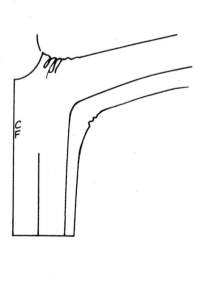

3. *Divided Gusset*

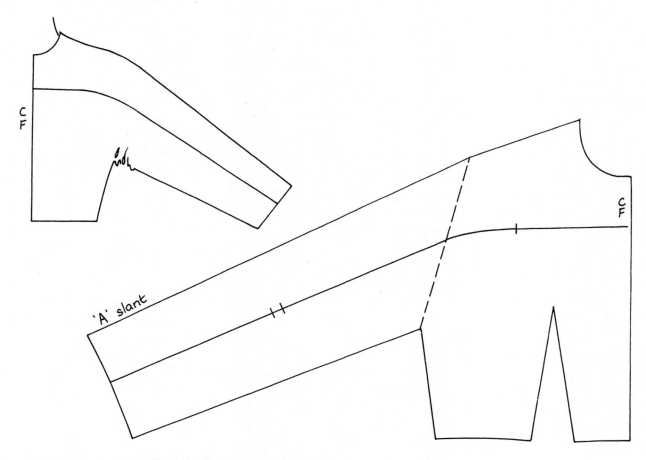

1. Draw in required dividing line and mark in notches. Cut along this line and arm hole line on lower section.
2. Open out the arm hole line and allow in extra for the under arm seam to return to its original length in basic block.
3. Smooth off top edge and under arm line. The latter must be identical at both front and back.

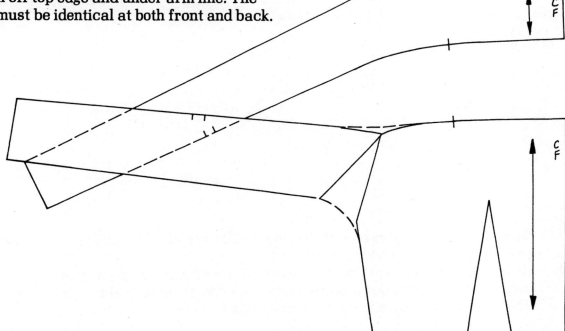

Batwing Sleeve

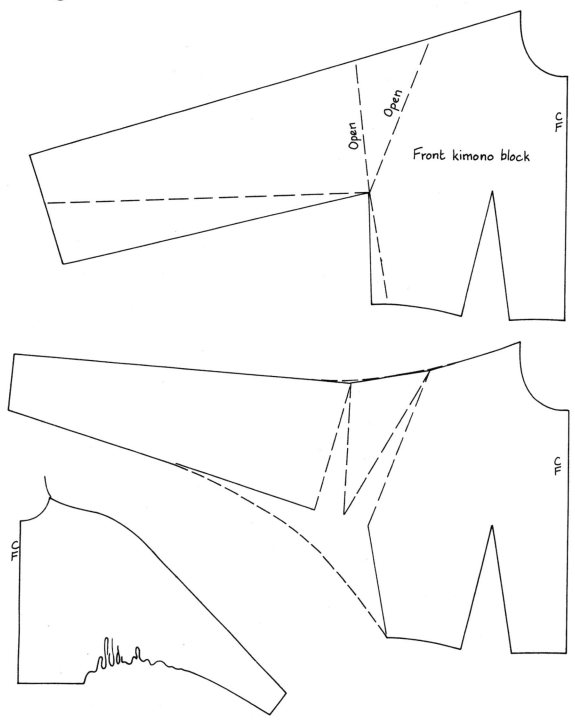

1. Take off 2 cm from side of waist on front and back blocks. Take off sufficient at wrist to give a more fitting wrist to sleeve.
2. Slash open from under arm point to shoulder and further down sleeve. Add any amount of fullness, in this under arm area, according to style and fabric. Ensure that back and front under arm seams are of the same length.

Magyar Sleeve

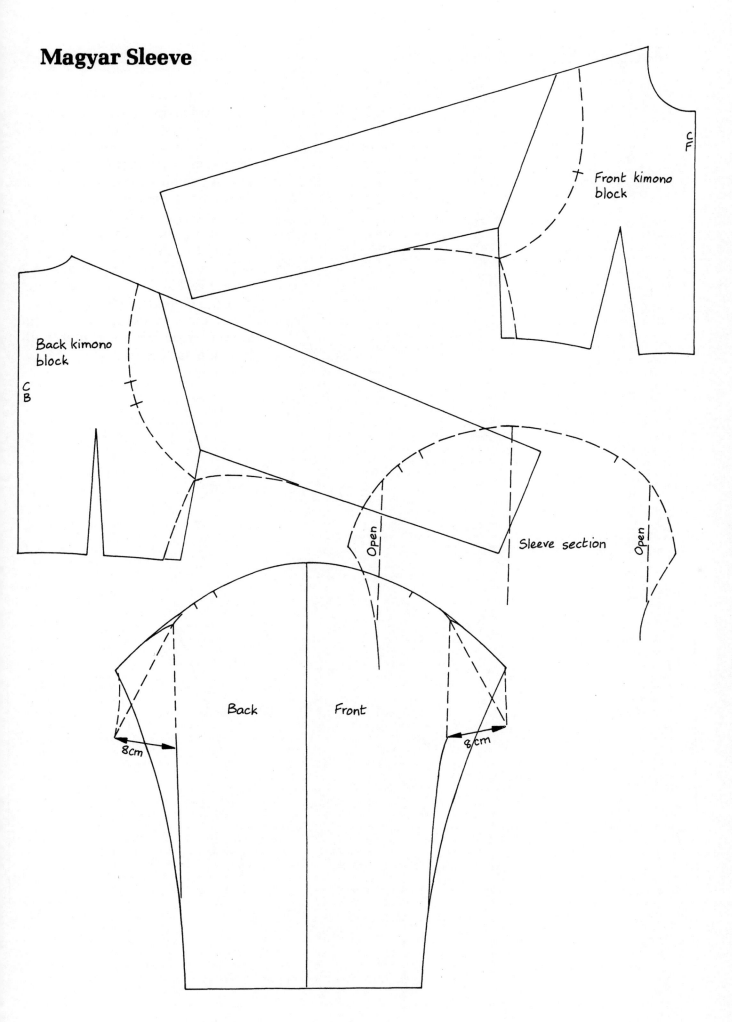

Front kimono block

CF

Back kimono block

CB

Open

Open

Sleeve section

Back

Front

8cm

8cm

Magyar Sleeve continued

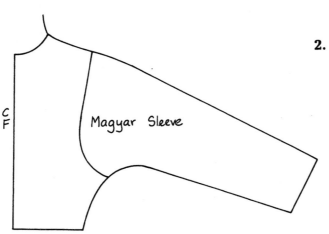

1. Draw in magyar seam line where required on basic Kimono blocks and remove the 2 cm (added during Kimono construction), from back and front waist at side seams. Notch seam lines.

2. Trace off front and back sleeve sections and unite into one sleeve pattern. To give extra length to under arm seam we need to open up the under arm area, as shown in diagram, approx. 8 cm. Draw in new under arm line, ensuring that both curved seam lines are identical in shape and length.

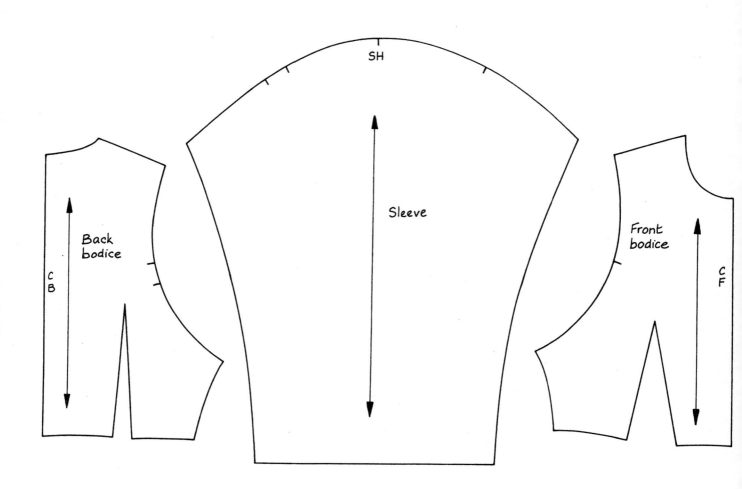

Square Arm Holes

Method 1

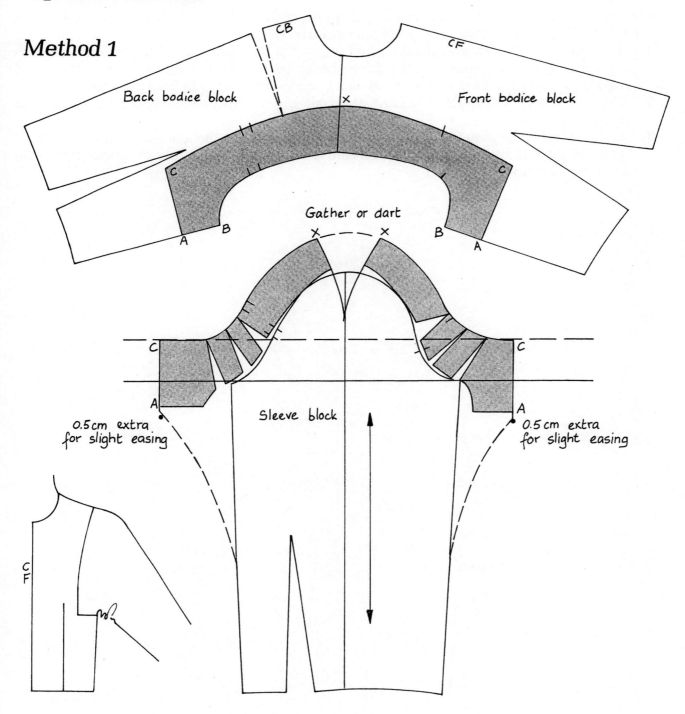

1. Line up blocks touching at shoulder and draw in square arm hole. Place balance notches half-way around new arm hole.
2. Draw a line above and parallel to the under arm line of the sleeve; the amount between A and B on bodice. Slash into arm hole until C lies smoothly on to the new line, when original arm hole notches are touching.
3. Curve a line from a point 0.5 cm below A to original sleeve, according to style, checking that each side is an equal shape and length. This extra 0.5 cm is eased into seam line.

Method 2

This method (based on the Kimono method) produces a basic fit more suitable for heavier fabrics and therefore jackets and coats particularly.

1. Line up blocks touching at shoulder and draw in square arm hole. Place balance notches C and D. Mark points A and B (which should be the same distance from the original under arm points). 0.5 cm past side seams to give slight easing in final pattern.

2. Place sleeve into arm hole touching at shoulder point and equidistant from under arm points.

3. Curve a line from A to C, B to D and cut open allowing in the amount dropped at under arm. Connect A and B back to original sleeve according to style, checking that each side is an equal shape.

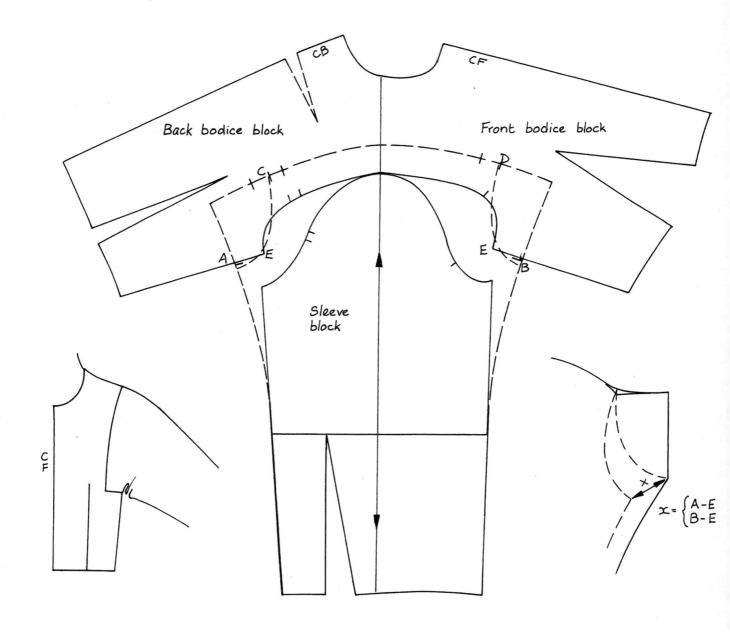

82

Pattern Pieces for Methods 1 and 2 Square Arm Holes

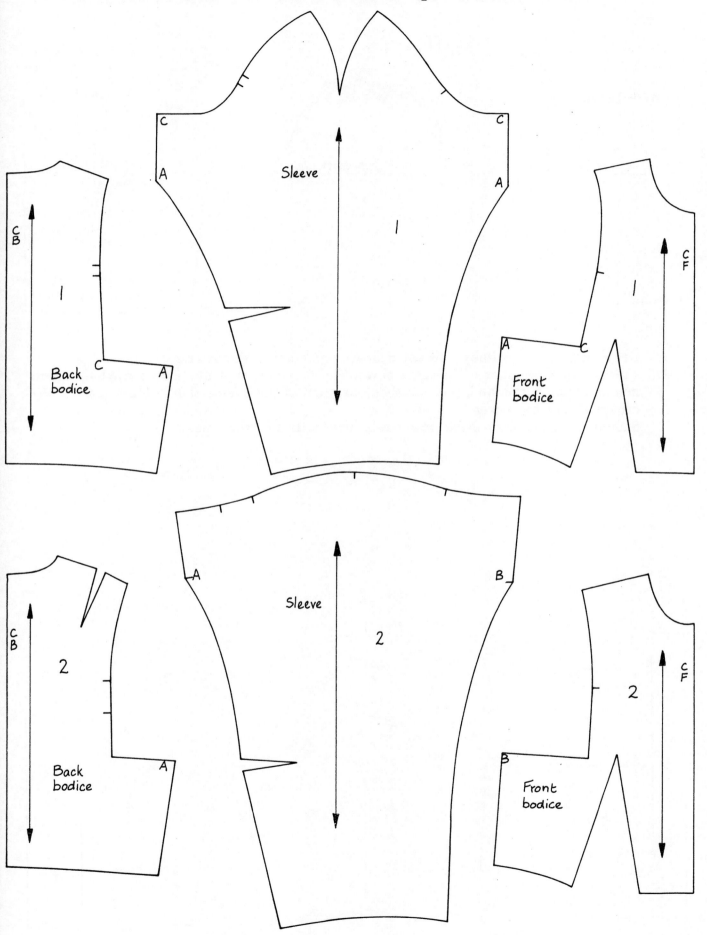

Dropped Shoulder Lines

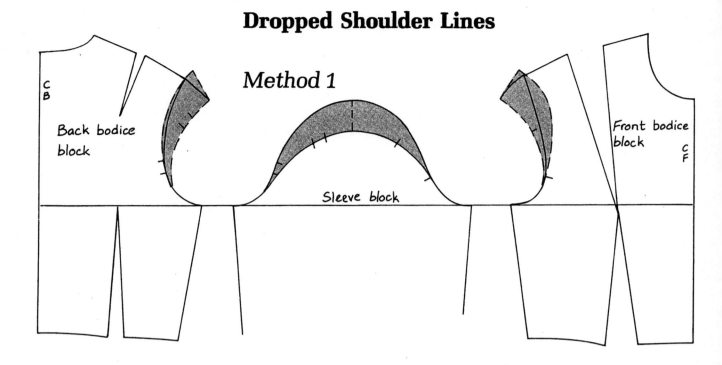

Method 1

Back bodice block

Sleeve block

Front bodice block

1. Draw required style line on crown of sleeve and notch new seam line.
2. Trace off these sections. These are now added to the appropriate bodice arm holes. Arm hole notches must match and the shoulder point of the bodice should touch part of the crown of the sleeve area.
3. Smooth off any uneven areas on shoulder lines with a curved line.

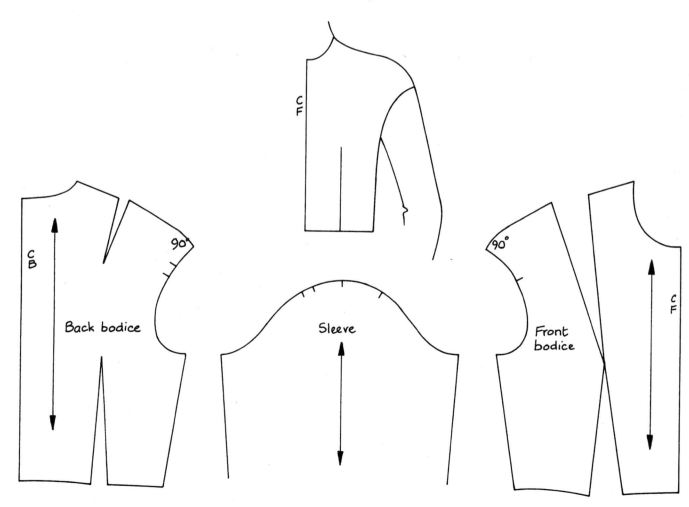

Method 2

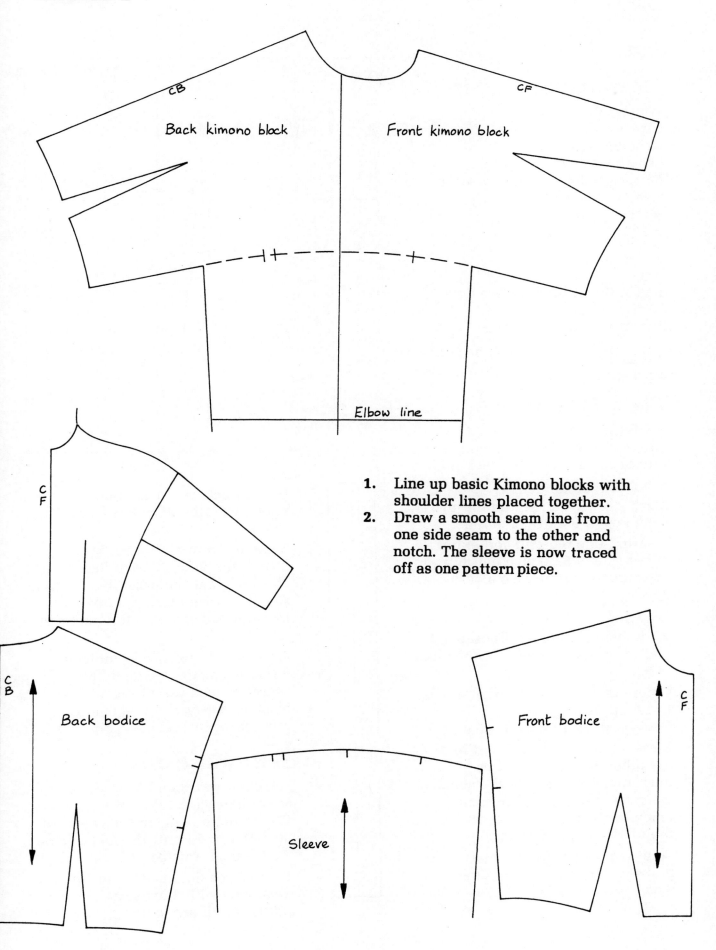

1. Line up basic Kimono blocks with shoulder lines placed together.
2. Draw a smooth seam line from one side seam to the other and notch. The sleeve is now traced off as one pattern piece.

Skirts

Skirt Block

Measurements—Size 12

Waist = 65 cm
Hips = 90 cm
Height = 163 cm
Length = 60 cm
Balance factor = ½ hips–½ waist ÷ 7
Size 12 balance factor
= (45 – 32.5) ÷ 7
= 12.5 ÷ 7 = 1.8 cm

Code

1 from 0 = ½ hips, square down from point 1

2 from 1 = balance factor

3 from 1 ⎫ skirt length (line 0–4 is
4 from 0 ⎬ squared down from line 0–2)

join 3 to 4 for hemline

5 is midway 1–0

6 from 2 = one-eighth height; square across to centre back line

8 is midway 6–7

Mark a construction line through 5–8 to point 9 on the hemline.

Measure line 6–7 and add extra either side of 8, to give half hip measurement plus 2.5 cm ease.

9–12 ⎫ 5 cm
9–13 ⎭

With identical curved lines join 10 and 11 to the two points either side of 8.

Continue with straight lines down to 12 and 13.

0–14 = balance factor + 0.5 cm

Measure 0–10 and 11–1 and find the difference between this measurement and ½ of the actual waist measurement. The surplus amount is made into two darts in the following proportions:

⅓ into front dart (positioned midway 5–1 and squared down 9 cm)

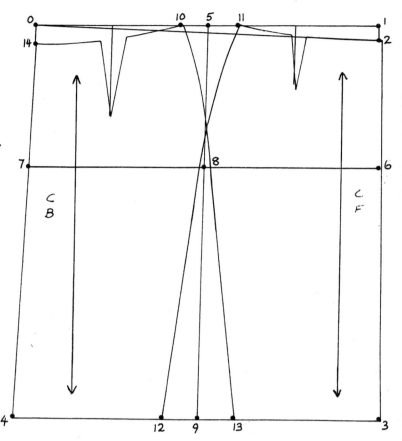

⅔ into back dart (positioned midway 0–10 and squared down 13 cm)

Trace off front and back skirt blocks and fold out each dart, checking that the waist line forms a smooth curve. Place side seams together and smooth off hemline at side seam.

Add seam allowance as indicated on page 3, cut out sample from calico for personal fitting. Adjust block to personal fitting before proceeding further.

Skirt waistband

Mark out waistband 5 cm wide by 65 cm long (size 12) plus 3 cm wrap. The dotted line down the centre of the band represents the fold line on the finished waistband.

Take off the final pattern for the waistband with 1 cm seam allowance all around.

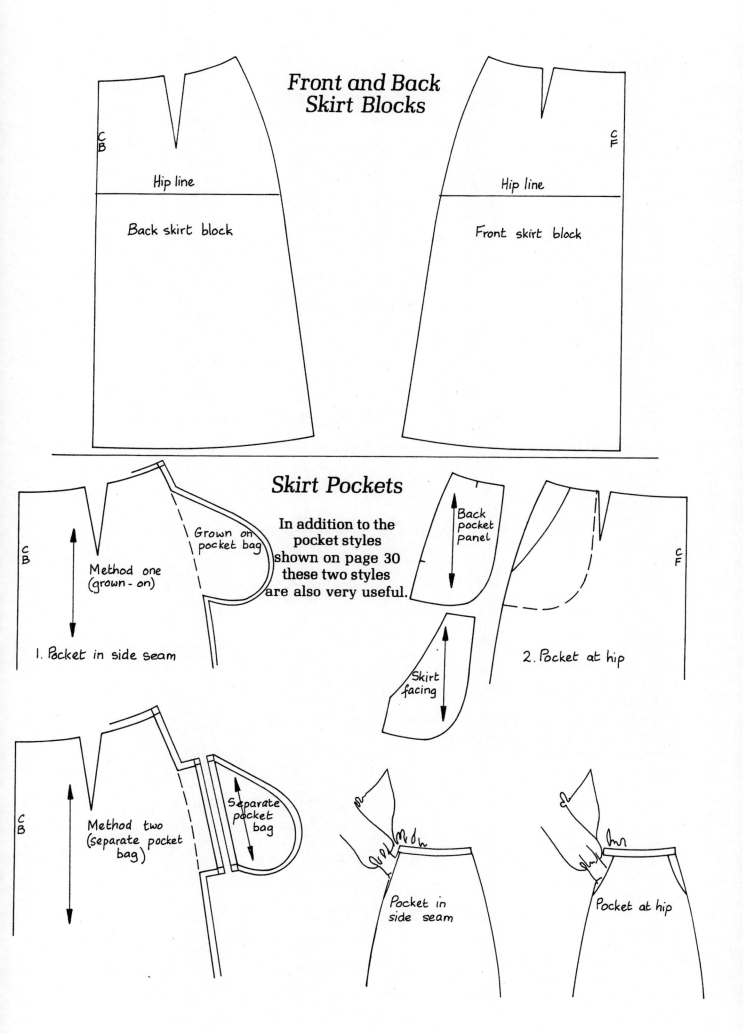

Front and Back Skirt Blocks

C
B

Hip line

Back skirt block

C
F

Hip line

Front skirt block

Skirt Pockets

In addition to the pocket styles shown on page 30 these two styles are also very useful.

C
B

Grown on pocket bag

Method one (grown - on)

1. Pocket in side seam

Back pocket panel

Skirt facing

C
F

2. Pocket at hip

C
B

Method two (separate pocket bag)

Separate pocket bag

Pocket in side seam

Pocket at hip

Circular Skirt

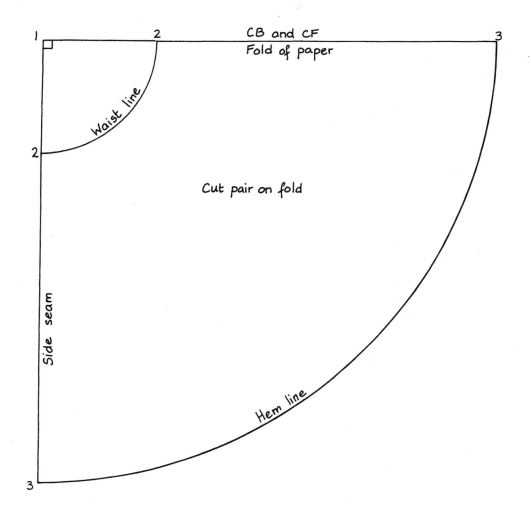

1–2 = $\frac{1}{6}$ waist measurement.

2–3 = skirt length.

Grain line can be through CB and CF or side seams depending on the width of the fabric to be used.

Semi-circular Skirt

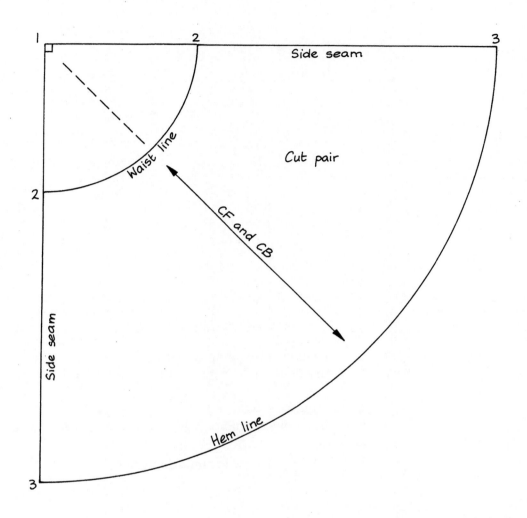

1–2 = $\frac{1}{3}$ waist measurement.
2–3 = skirt length.
Grain line can also be positioned at side seam if required.

Culotte Skirt

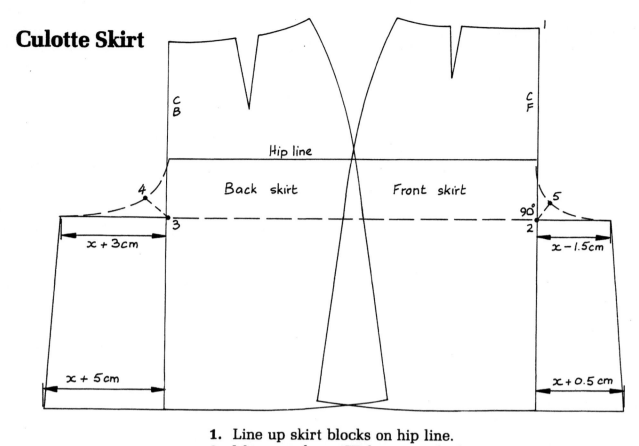

1. Line up skirt blocks on hip line.
2. Measure down CF from 1 to find 2 (1−2 = body rise + 1.5 cm).
3. Square across from 2 to 3.
4. $x = \frac{1}{8}$ hip measurement. Make necessary additions as on diagram.

   $\left.\begin{matrix} 3-4 = 4 \text{ cm} \\ 2-5 = 3 \text{ cm} \end{matrix}\right\}$ Draw in smooth curves.

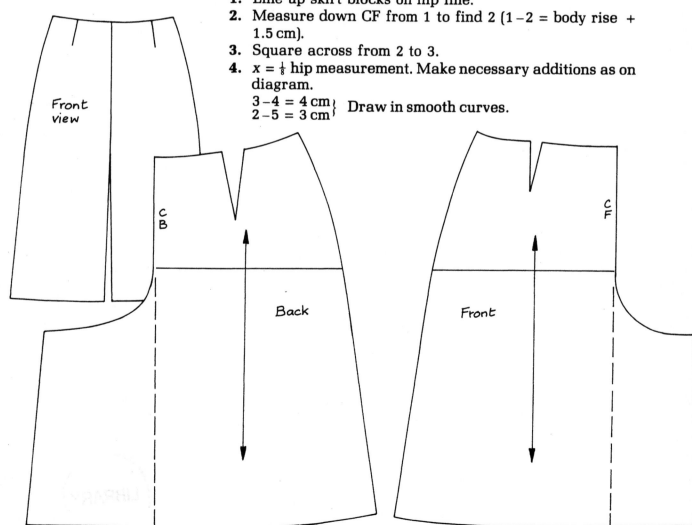

Flared Panelled Skirt

Eight Panel Skirt

$1-2 = \frac{1}{8}$ waist measurement
+ 2 cm ease. [For size
12 this would be
$(65 + 2) \div 8 = 8.375$ cm

$3-4 = \frac{1}{8}$ hip measurement
+ 4 cm ease. [For
size 12 this would be
$(90 + 4) \div 8 = 11.75$ cm

$\left.\begin{array}{l}1-5 \\ 2-6\end{array}\right\} =$ skirt length.

Add flare according to
style.
Waist shape may need to
be refined
at a later stage.

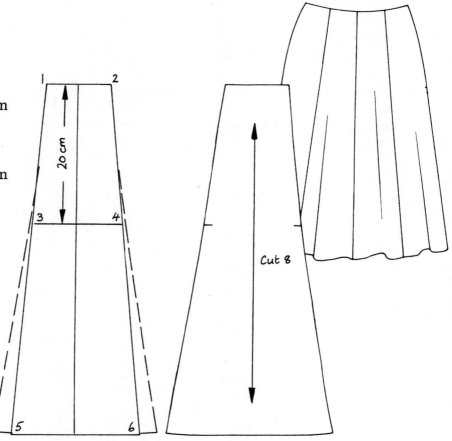

Six Panel Skirt

$1-2 = \frac{1}{6}$ hip measurement
+ 2 cm ease. (For size
12 this would be
$(65 + 2) \div 6 = 11.2$ cm

$3-4 = \frac{1}{6}$ hip measurement
+ 4 cm ease. [For
size 12 this would be
$(90 + 4) \div 6 = 15.7$ cm

$\left.\begin{array}{l}1-5 \\ 2-6\end{array}\right\} =$ skirt length.

Add flare according to
style.
Waist shape may need to
be refined at a later
stage.

N.B. This method of
dividing up the waist and
hip measurements, with
the required ease will
work for any number of
panels.

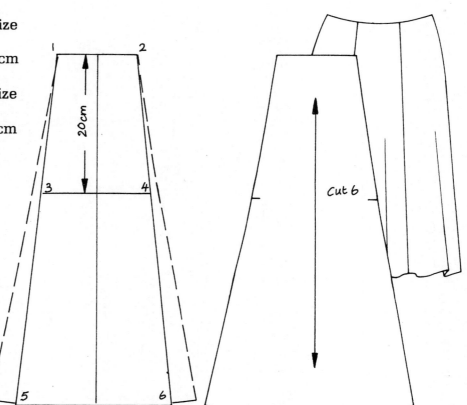

Skirt with Yoke and Unpressed Pleats

1. Line up skirt blocks on hip line.
2. Mark in yoke seam and divide front sections (below yoke seam) into four panels. Position notches on yoke seam line.
3. Trace off lower skirt sections and open out to required shape. Mark in tuck positions and draw around new skirt shape.

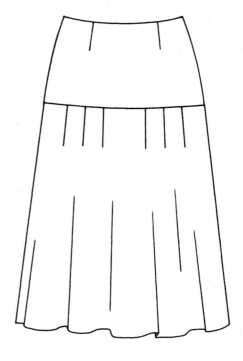

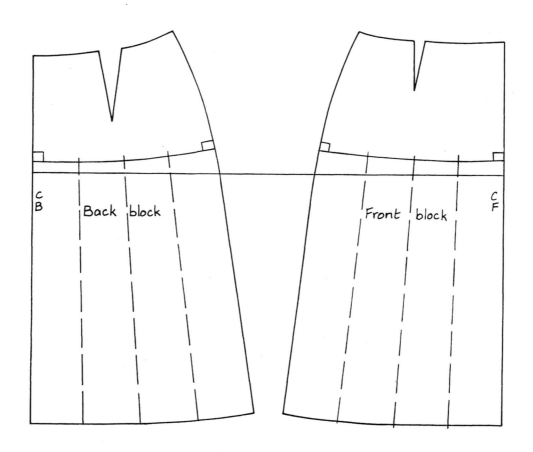

Back block

Front block

C B

C F

Skirt with Yoke and Unpressed Pleats continued

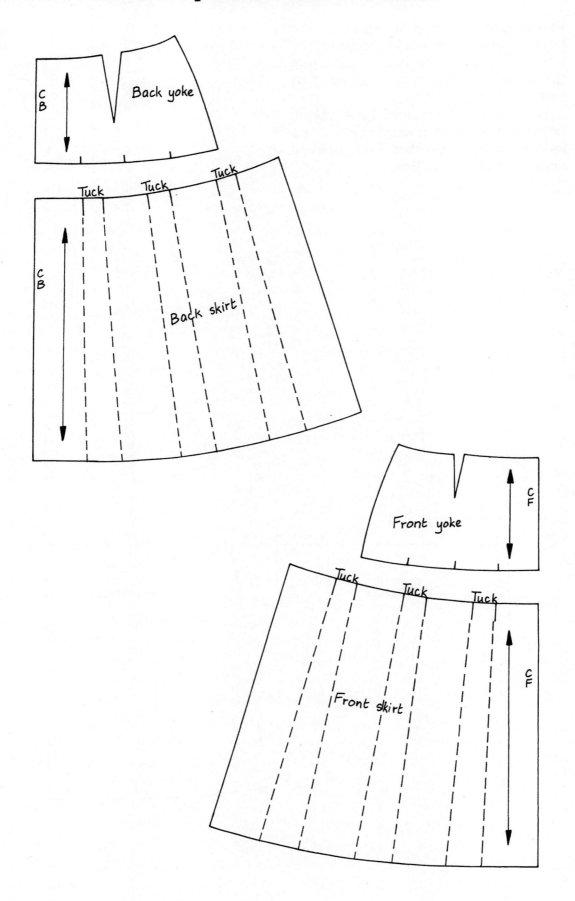

Flared Skirt with Shaped Yoke

1. Line up skirt blocks on hip line.
2. Mark in yoke and position notches.
3. Divide front and back, below yokes, into three sections. Trace off and open at hem line as required.
4. Close darts in front and back yokes; continue front dart down to yoke seam before closing. Smooth off any uneven areas on styled seam lines.

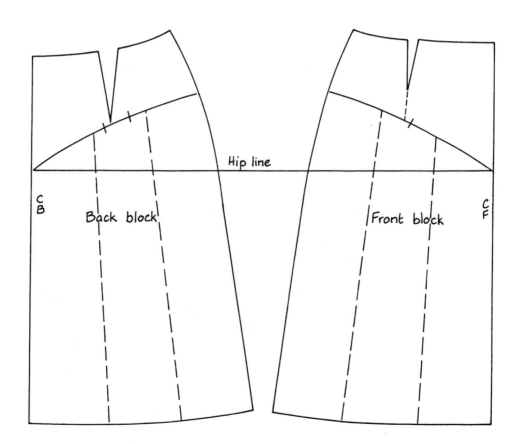

Hip line

C
B

Back block

Front block

C
F

Flared Skirt with Shaped Yoke continued

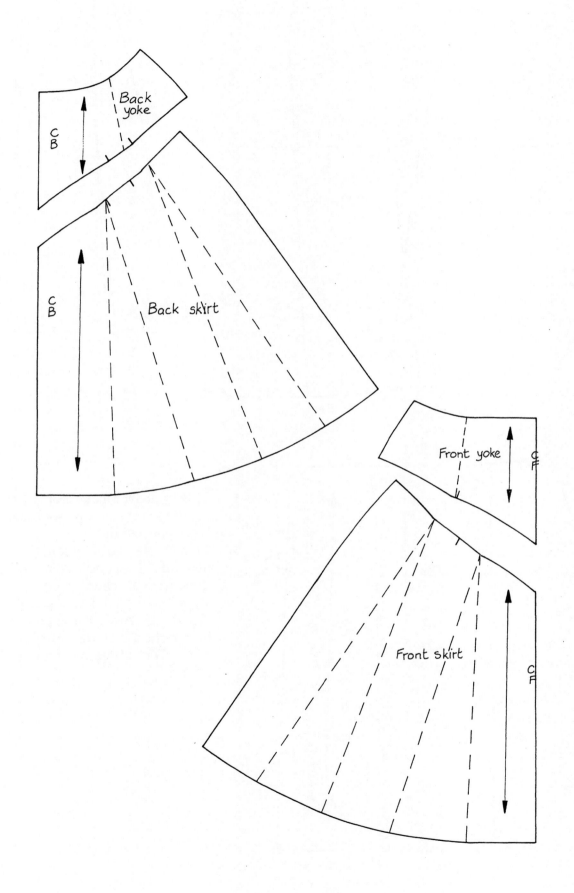

Skirt with Two Inverted Front Pleats

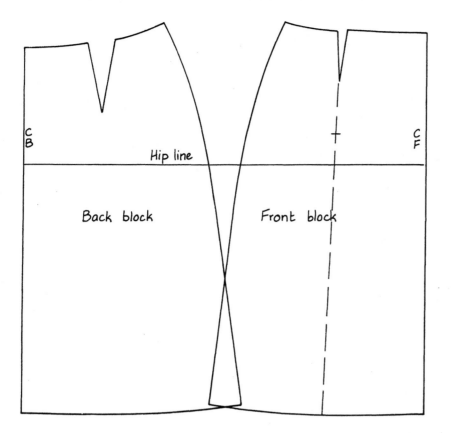

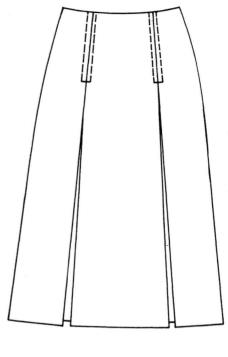

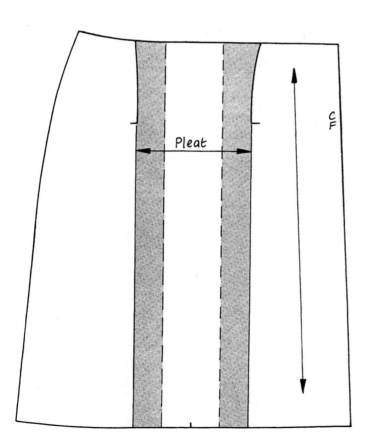

1. Line up skirt blocks on hip line.
2. Divide front into two sections down from point of dart.
3. Trace off both sections. Draw around CF section and add pleat allowance depending on fabric and style. Add side front panel. From the notch upwards the pleat should be stitched together to remove the dart. Top stitching may also be added.

Skirt with CF Box Pleat

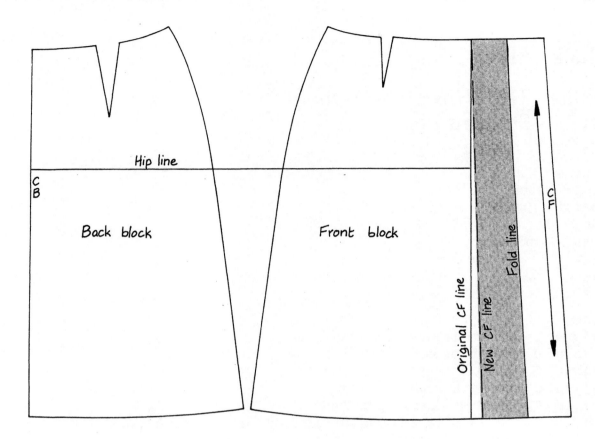

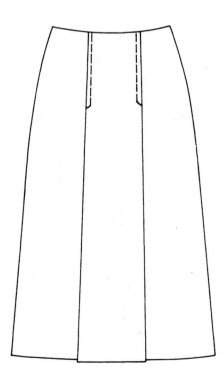

1. Line up blocks on hip line.
2. Add 1 – 1.5 cm to hem at CF to avoid pleat gaping.
3. Add pleat allowance, according to fabric and style, on to new CF line. Make the pleat slightly wider at the hem than at the waist.
4. Top stitch the pleat as a means of support and decoration.

Ladies' Slacks

Slacks Block

Scale—Half Hip Measurement
Style—Straight Legs
Measurements—Size 12

Waist = 65 cm.
Hips = 90 cm.
Body rise = 27 cm.
Inleg = 84 cm.
Height = 163 cm.
Hem width = 48 cm.

Code

Front

 0 from 1 = Body rise plus 1.5 cm tolerance.
 2 from 0 = Half inleg minus 5 cm knee line.
 3 from 0 = Inleg.
 4 from 0 = one-sixth scale plus 1 cm.
 5 from 4 = one-twelfth scale plus 2 cm.
    6 is located on a dotted line squared from four to the waist line.
 7 from 6 = one-eight height.
 8 from 6 = 1 cm.
 9 from 4 = 2 cm, at a 45° angle, shape 5–9–7–8.
10 from 8 = Quarter waist plus 1.5 cm dart value.
11 from 7 = Half scale.
12 from 3 = one-quarter hem width minus 5 mm. ⎫
13 from 3 = one-quarter hem width minus 5 mm. ⎭ Square up to knee line
A from 10 = 7 cm. A is the centre of a 1.5 cm dart.
Trace of front:
Mark grain line 1 to 3, fold out dart and reshape waist lines.

Back

14 from 5 = one-twelfth scale plus 1 cm, square down.
15 from 14 = 1 cm.
16 from 8 = 3 cm, draw in back seat angle 7–16, continue line 4 cm past 16 to 17.
18 from 11 = 2 cm.
19 from 12 = 1 cm square up to knee line.
20 from 13 = 1 cm.
21 from 17 = one-quarter waist, shape back as indicated in diagram.
22 from 15 = 15 cm.

To complete back block

Mark grain line 1 to 3; and
Mark on block, that the areas 7 to 15 and 15 to 22 are to be stretched when sewn.

Block

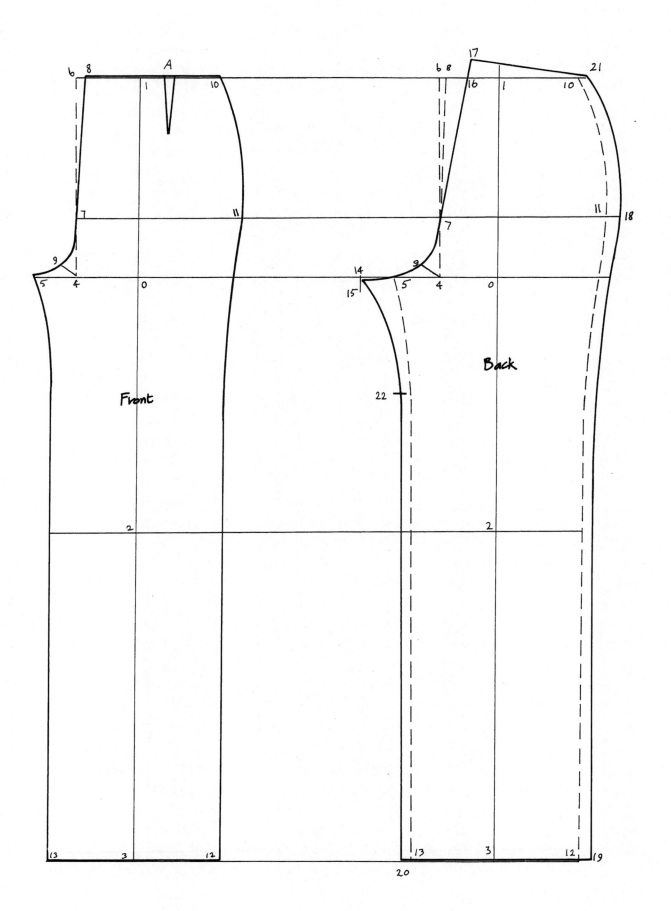

Front

Back

Slacks Block continued

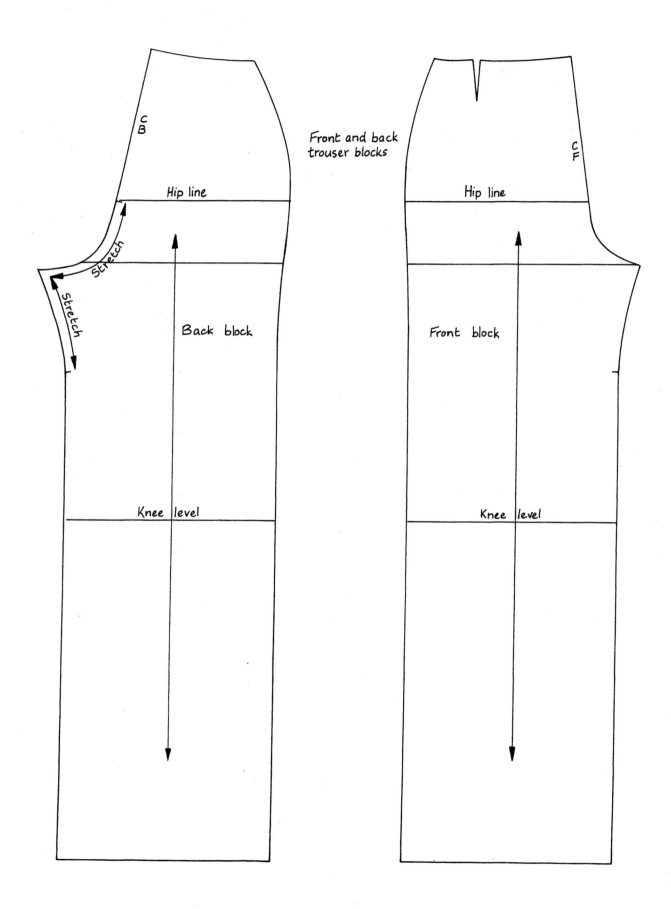

C
B

Front and back
trouser blocks

C
F

Hip line

Hip line

Stretch

Stretch

Back block

Front block

Knee level

Knee level

Slacks Variations

1. 'Oxford Bags'

1. Lower crutch by 1.5 cm and move out 1.5 cm.
2. Straighten off outside and inside leg.
3. Draw in shaped waist band and join into one curved band.
4. Slash front trouser where tucks are required; open amount for depth of tuck at top edge but keep hem area together.
5. Draw in fly extension from a point 2 cm below where zip is to finish. As well as this extension make one separate pattern piece of this section to be used as a facing.

See pattern pieces on page 103.

C B

Slash

Slash

C F

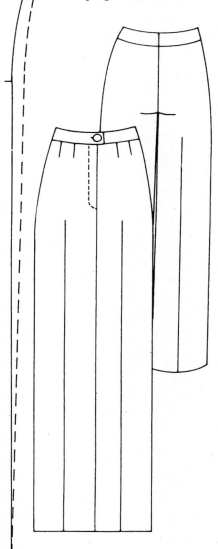

2. *Slimfitting Jeans*

1. Make legs narrower from mid thigh to hem.
2. Draw in shaped waist band and join into one piece.
3. Draw in desired yoke and pocket shapes on back.
4. From level where back yoke meets side seam, begin front pocket, ensuring a hand can easily fit. Draw in line of pocket bag.
5. Draw in zip fly extension from a point 2 cm below where zip is to finish. As well as this extension make one separate pattern piece of this section to be used as a facing.

   See pattern pieces on page 103.

Pattern Pieces

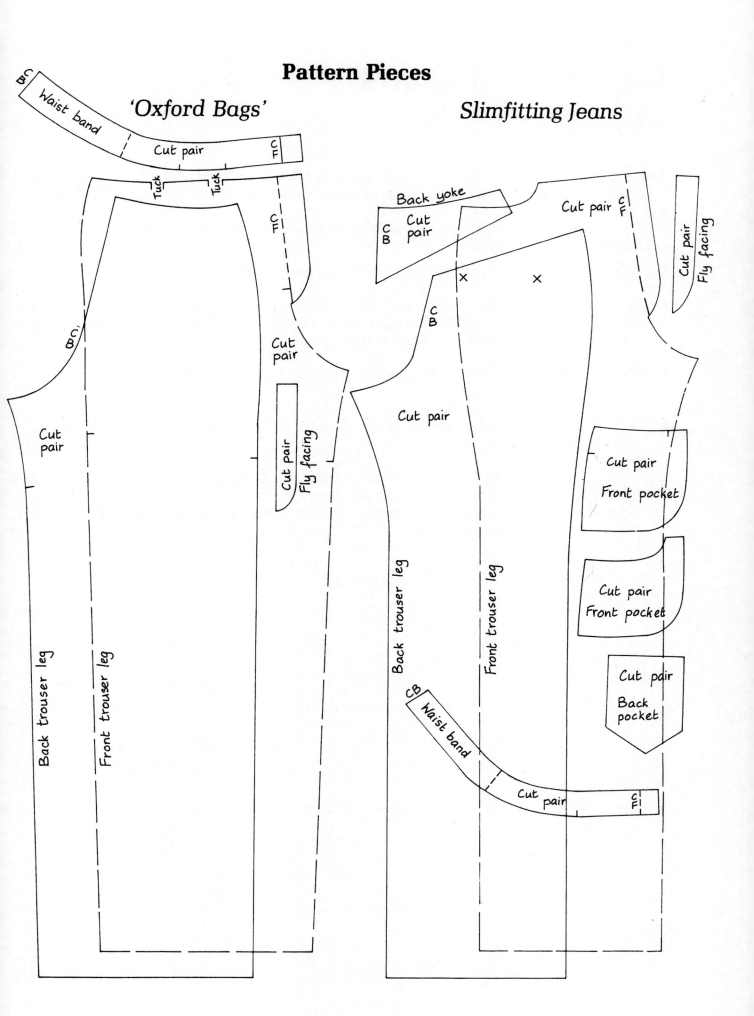

'Oxford Bags'

Waist band
B C
Cut pair
C F

Tuck   Tuck
C F

Cut pair

B C

Cut pair

Cut pair
Fly facing

Back trouser leg

Front trouser leg

Slimfitting Jeans

Back yoke
C B Cut pair

Cut pair
C F

Cut pair
Fly facing

C B

Cut pair

Cut pair
Front pocket

Cut pair
Front pocket

Cut pair
Back pocket

Back trouser leg

Front trouser leg

C B
Waist band
Cut pair
C F

Jackets and Coats

Introduction

The blocks on the following pages should serve only as a guide and each particular jacket and coat design must be treated individually; nevertheless the following are useful basic blocks.

The following points should be considered when sizing up the dress block to a jacket or coat block:

1. What is the style of garment—e.g. tailored, flared or tubular?

2. Is the garment to be worn over much indoor clothing? If so, allow for particular features on certain kinds of garments—i.e. a fitted dress with shawl collar, a chunky jumper with a large polo collar or a blouse with full batwing sleeves.

3. What is the nature and weight of the chosen fabric for the design—e.g. wool velour, silk, corduroy or linen?

4. Is canvas required in any areas? Is the shoulder line to be soft and natural or square and padded?

5. If the garment is to be lined, what type of lining would be used—e.g. plain or quilted? Remember that the nature, weight and quality of the jacket or coat fabric usually determines whether the garment should be lined or not, as well as the chosen market and price the garment is aimed at.

Basic Jacket Block

Back

1. Raise back neck point 0.5 cm.

2. Raise shoulder point 0.5 cm and move out 0.5 cm (giving an easier fitting shoulder seam section).

3. Shoulder pad allowance if required taken only to mid shoulder – allow 0.5 in height from 2, as thickest part of pad only reaches to mid shoulder; the seam will therefore appear to be curved, which is correct. Make a note on the block stating how much shoulder pad allowance has been added if any.

4. Add 0.5 cm across half back.

5. Drop under arm point 1 cm and move out 1 cm.

6. Move out 1 cm and connect to 5, rounding at waist line.

7. Reduce waist 1 cm at CB, off to nothing at approximately under arm level, and possibly flaring out a little at hemline.

8. Drop dart point 2.5 cm; darts which are too long often give unprofessional results.

   Draw in new chest line 1 cm below the original.

Front

9. Lower front neckline 1 cm.

10. Raise neck 0.5 cm and move out 0.5 cm.

11. Reduce dart on neck side by 0.5 cm.

12. Raise shoulder point 0.5 cm and move out 0.5 cm to correspond with back.

13. Allow 0.5 cm in height from point 12 (as for back shoulder point).

14. Add 0.5 cm to chest.

15. Drop under arm point 1 cm and move out 1 cm.

16. Move out 1 cm, connect to 15, using back side seam as a guide if a shoulder pad allowance is required.

17. Add 0.5 cm to front waist level, connect to neck point with a straight line, then continue down to hem level (this ensures that hem level does not gape at CF). This now becomes the new CF line.

18. Shorten shoulder and waist darts by moving away from bust point by 2 cm each side.

19. Mark 0.5 cm on either side of lower point of dart and continue two lines down to hem line.

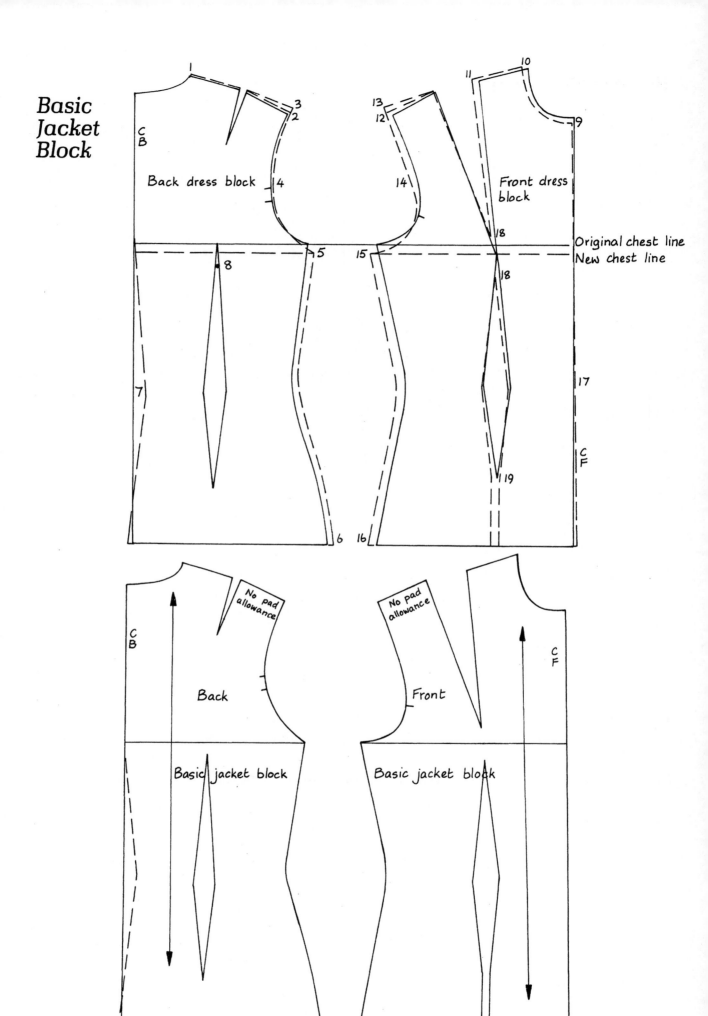

Basic Jacket Block

Back dress block

Front dress block

Original chest line
New chest line

No pad allowance

Back

Basic jacket block

No pad allowance

Front

Basic jacket block

Basic Jacket Sleeve Block

Outline the basic sleeve block, marking in all the guide lines.

1. Raise sleeve head 0.5 cm to correspond with alteration to shoulder point on jacket block.

2. Raise crown another 0.5 cm if shoulder pads are to be used; make a note on the block stating how much shoulder pad allowance has been added, if any.

3. Move mid-crown out 0.5 cm on either side; this gives extra width across the upper arm for easier movement and allows for a lining if it is to be used.

4. Move back under arm point down 1 cm and out 1.5 cm; this extra 0.5 cm allowed into the base of the back arm hole of the sleeve is eased into the jacket arm hole to give an easier fit when arms are moved forwards. Continue 1.5 cm down to hem.

5. Move front arm hole point down 1 cm and out 1 cm. Continue 1 cm down to hem.

6. Lengthen sleeve by 1 cm.

Draw in the new sleeve head and place balance notches to correspond with the jacket block. This sleeve may be used to construct a two-piece tailored sleeve which would give a more smooth, tailored line.

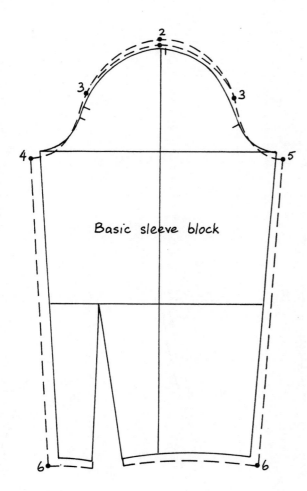

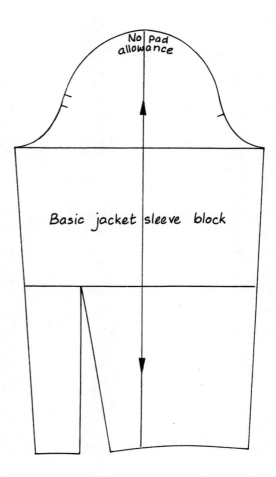

Two-piece Tailored Sleeve

1. Fold out elbow dart.

2. Fold sleeve so that the under arm seams touch the centre line. Use sticky tape to join these seams together. Measure in from the two fold lines 2.5 cm at under arm level and 1 cm at the wrist. Connect these points to give seam lines. Place notches either side of elbow line, approx. 16 cm on front of sleeve and 8 cm on back.

3. Cut along elbow line and pivot from centre grain line; swing 2 cm into the back sleeve length and therefore reducing the front sleeve edge, and secure with sticky tape.

4. Cut along new seam lines and mark the areas of stretching and easing.

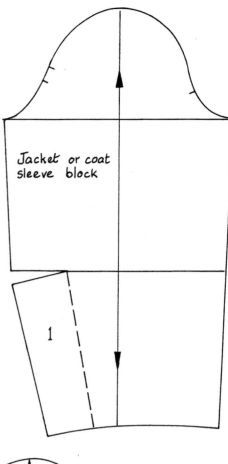

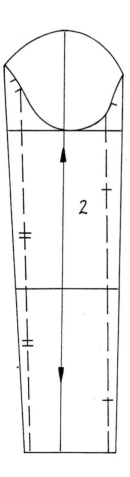

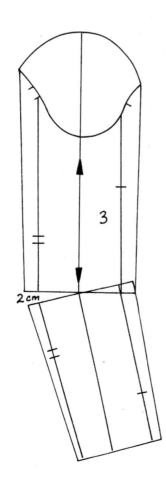

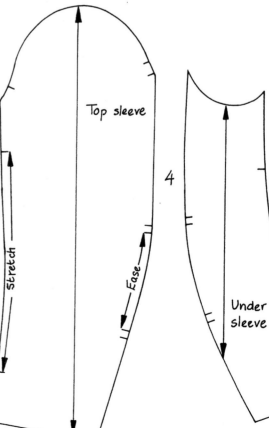

Jacket Styles

1.

1. Line up blocks on new chest line with arm hole points touching.

2. The CB seam is slightly fitted.

3. The back panel is taken from the back arm hole in a good line through to the hem—this panel includes the waist suppression of back dart.

4. The side seam is moved forward 2 cm and transformed into a dart.

5. Swing front shoulder dart into a smooth curved line from arm hole to bust point.

6. Smooth off any angles on seam lines and draw in appropriate collar button wrap etc.

See pattern pieces on page 111.

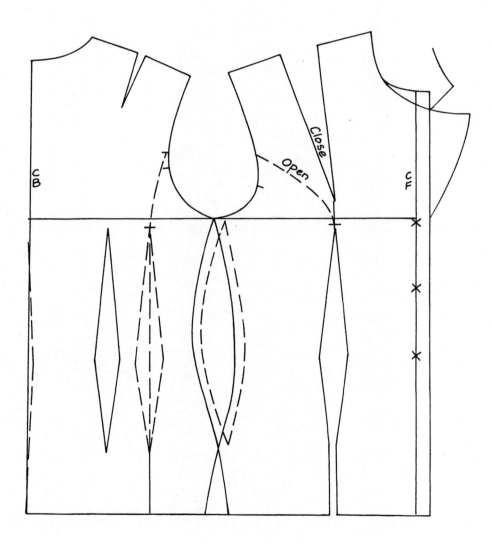

2.

1. Line up blocks on new chest line.

2. The back panel is taken from the shoulder to the hem incorporating both the shoulder and waist dart.

3. The front panel is taken through the shoulder dart, down to the hem, incorporating the front waist dart.
   It is possible to take all the waist suppression out on the side panel, as shown on the front jacket, leaving a straight seam on the centre front panel—this is necessary when producing a double-breasted style of jacket. The volume of the shaded area forms a small dart through the centre of the front side panel.

4. Smooth off any angles on new seam lines and draw in the appropriate collar and double breasted extension etc.

See pattern on page 111.

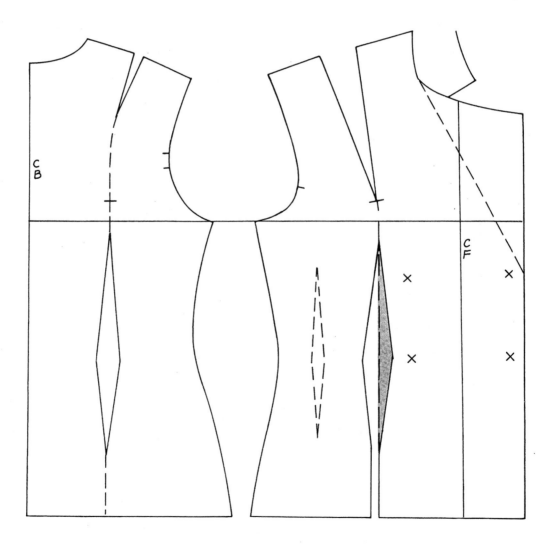

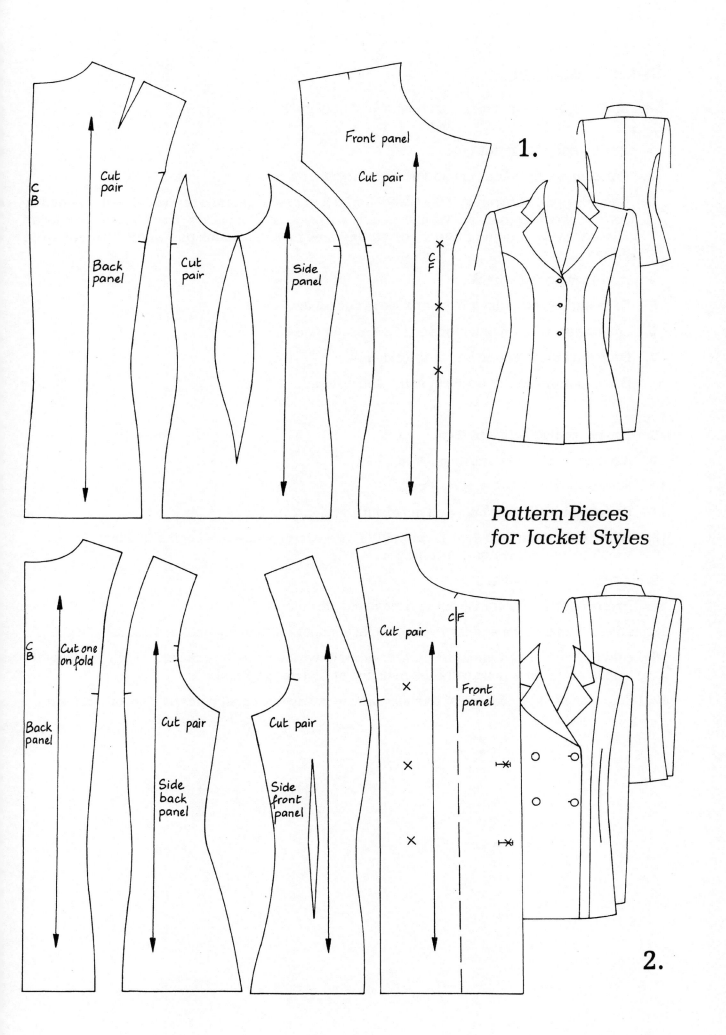

C B

Cut pair

Back panel

Cut pair

Side panel

Front panel

Cut pair

C F

1.

Pattern Pieces for Jacket Styles

C B

Cut one on fold

Back panel

Cut pair

Side back panel

Cut pair

Side front panel

Cut pair

C F

Front panel

2.

Basic Coat Block

Line up dress blocks and mark in chest, waist and hip lines.

Back

1. Raise back neck point 1 cm.

2. Raise shoulder point 1 cm and move out 1 cm.

3. Shoulder pad allowance if required; add 0.5 – 1 cm (depending on size of pad) to point 2. As the shoulder pad allowance is only taken to mid shoulder, the seam will appear curved. Make a note on the block stating how much shoulder pad allowance has been added, if any.

4. Add 1 cm across $\frac{1}{2}$ back.

5. Drop under arm point 1.5 cm and move out 1.5 cm.

6. Lower hem by 2 cm and move out 1.5 cm; connect to 5.

7. Drop dart point 1.5 cm below the original.

   Draw in new chestline 1.6 cm below the original.

Front

8. Lower front neckline by 2 cm.

9. Raise neck 1 cm and move out 1 cm.

10. Reduce dart on neck side by 1 cm.

11. Raise shoulder point 1 cm and move out 1 cm.

12. Allow 0.5 – 1 cm in height from point 11 (to correspond with back shoulder) if a shoulder pad allowance is required.

13. Add 1 cm across chest.

14. Drop under arm point 1.5 cm and move out 1.5 cm.

15. Lower hem by 2 cm and move out 1.5 cm; connect to 14, using back side seam as a guide.

16. Add 0.5 cm to front waist level; connect to 8 with a straight line then continue down to hem level. (This is to prevent the hem line at CF from gaping.)

17. Shorten shoulder and waist darts by moving away from bust point by 2 cm on each side.

Basic Coat Block

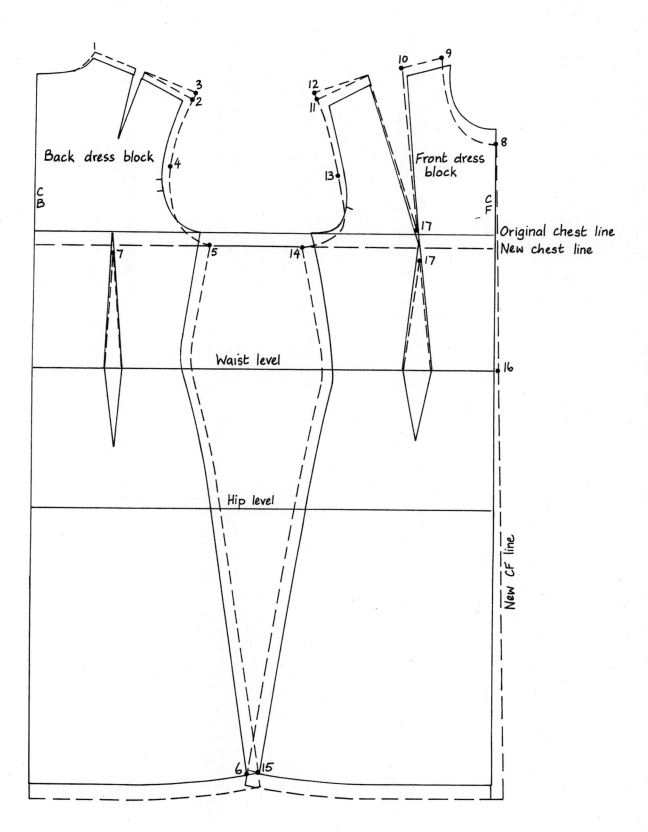

Back dress block

Front dress block

Original chest line
New chest line

Waist level

Hip level

New CF line

Basic Coat Block continued

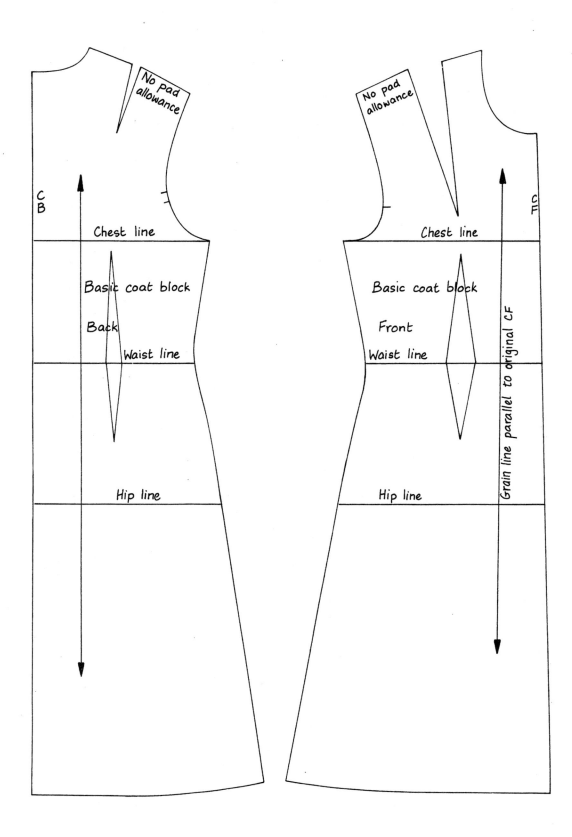

No pad allowance

C B

Chest line

Basic coat block

Back

Waist line

Hip line

No pad allowance

C F

Chest line

Basic coat block

Front

Waist line

Grain line parallel to original CF

Hip line

Basic Coat Sleeve Block

Outline the basic sleeve block, marking in all the guide lines.

1. Raise sleeve head 1 cm to correspond with alteration to shoulder point on coat block.

2. Raise crown another 0.5 – 1 cm if shoulder pads are to be used. Make a note on block stating how much shoulder pad allowance has been added, if any.

3. Move mid-crown out 1 cm on either side; this gives extra width across the upper arm for easier movement and allows for a lining if it is to be used.

4. Move back under arm point down 1.5 cm and out 2 cm; this extra 0.5 cm allowed into the base of the back arm hole of the sleeve is eased into the coat arm hole to give an easier fit when arms are moved forwards. Continue 2 cm down to hem.

5. Move front arm hole point down 1.5 cm and out 1.5 cm. Continue 1.5 cm down to hem.

6. Lengthen sleeve by 1 – 1.5 cm.

Draw in the new sleeve head and place balance notches to corrrespond with the coat block. This sleeve may be used to construct a two-piece tailored sleeve which would give a more smooth, tailored line.

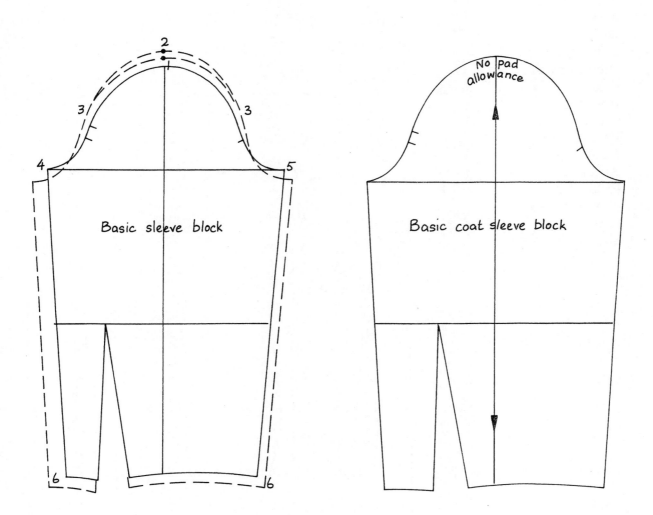

Jacket and Coat Linings and Facings

1. Facing shapes are drawn around back neck line, front edge and neck line no narrower than 7 cm; these would be interfaced.

2. 1 cm ease is put through front and back.

3. Arm hole is raised the amount of seam allowance used on coat or jacket.

4. The back shoulder dart forms a tuck and the front shoulder dart is swung into the front edge.

5. Add extra at CB to form a pleat—for ease of movement.

6. Shorten hem by 1–3 cm.

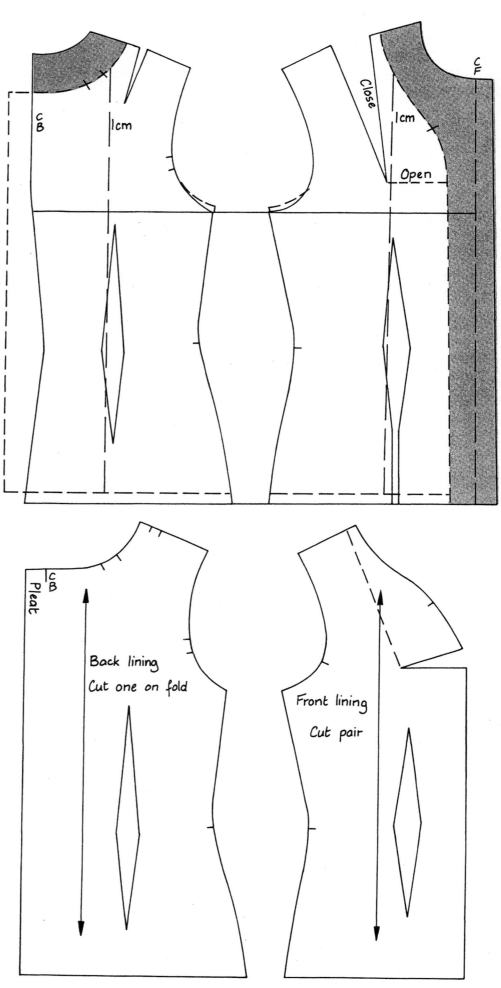

Back lining
Cut one on fold

Front lining
Cut pair

Underwear

Basic Bra Block

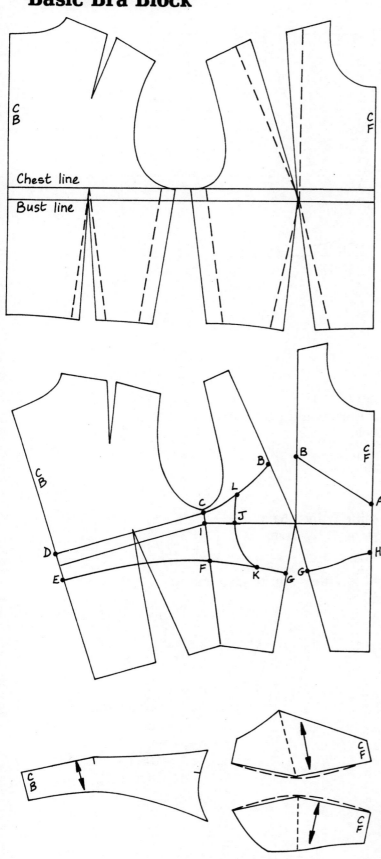

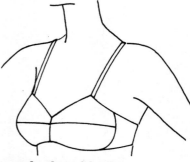

1. Line up bodice blocks and remove 2 cm tolerance from each side seam.
2. Mark on bust line, parallel to the chest line.
3. Double the volume of the waist darts and front shoulder dart.
4. Trace new bodice outlines, including bust line, and place side seams together.
   Mark on these points:
   A = 2.5 cm above bust line.
   B = 9 cm above bust line.
   C and D = 1.5 cm above bust line.
   E = 2 cm below bust line.
   F = 5 cm below bust line.
   G = 7 cm below bust line.
   H = 4 cm below bust line.
   I–J = 4 cm.
   C–L = 5 cm.
   F–K = 6.5 cm.
5. Join these points together as on centre diagram, and position a notch on line L–K at bust level.
6. Trace off back section up to line L–K, closing back dart. Trace off cup sections, swinging darts into the horizontal bust line to form two pieces; curve this cup seam line to give a more natural shape. Mark in grain lines parellel to CF and CB. Shoulder straps: the measurement between point B and shoulder and the corresponding amount on the back block are added together to give a guide, but this is usually reduced by 2–4 cm.

N.B. It should be noted that this is a very basic block which will require further styling and fitting according to the wearer's shape and size.

Basic French Knicker Block for Stretch Fabric

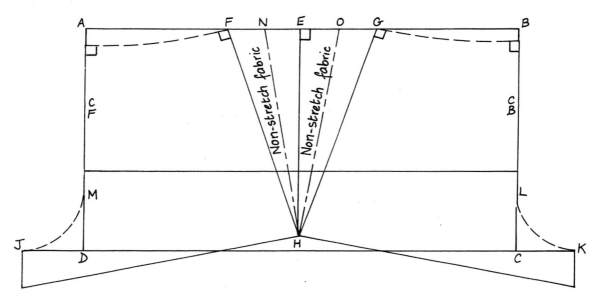

A–B = 12 cm plus $\frac{1}{2}$ hip measurement.

A–D and BC = body rise plus 4 cm.

D–C = A–B.

E = midway A to B.

F and G = 10 cm either side of E.

E–H = body rise plus 2 cm. Join F to H and G to H

Waist curvature allowance – drop waist at A 2 cm and 1.5 cm at B.

Join these points to F and G in smooth lines.

D–J and C–K = $\frac{1}{12}$ full hip measurement.

Square down from J and K, 5 cm leg length.

Join these two points to H.

C–L and D–M = 8 cm.

CF line—Join J to M in a smooth line, missing D by 3.5 cm.

CB line—Join K to L in a smooth line, missing C by 3 cm.

Draw in hip line 20 cm below line A to B.

Trace off front and back sections and join at side seam to give one pattern piece. Shape hem line as diagram.

See pattern piece on page 121.

Adaptation for non-stretch fabric

A–N $\left.\right\}$ = $\frac{1}{4}$ hip.
B–O $\left.\right\}$

Join to H.

118

Pantie Block for Non-stretch Fabric

Using Non-stretch French Knicker Blocks

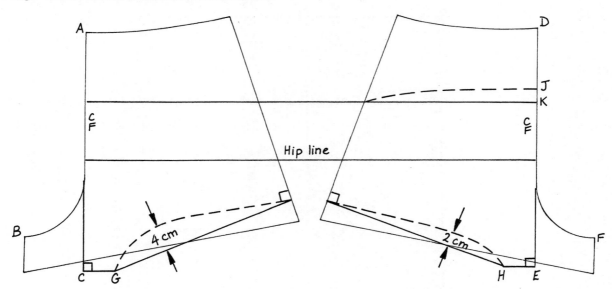

Line up blocks on hip line.

A–C = A–B.

D–E = D–F.

Shorten side seams by 3 cm from hem line.

$\left.\begin{array}{l} \text{C–G} \\ \text{E–H} \end{array}\right\}$ = 4 cm.

Connect G and H to new side seam points and draw in leg line in a smooth curve as in diagram.

For Hipster Briefs

Draw in new lower hip line.

D–J = 8 cm.

D–K = 10 cm.

Square across to CB from K and draw in top edge of panties as in diagram.

Trace off front and back sections and place side seams together. Smooth off top edge and leg edge.

Do not make into one section as in French knickers.

See pattern pieces on page 121.

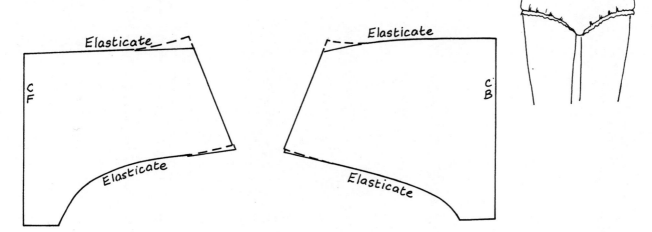

Pantie Block for Stretch Fabric

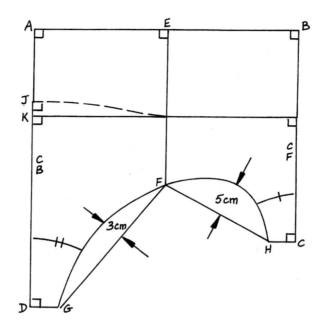

A–B = ½ waist + 4 cm.
A–D = body rise + 12 cm.
B–C = body rise + 3 cm.
   E = midway A–B.
E–F = body rise less 6 cm.
$\left.\begin{matrix} \text{D–G} \\ \text{C–H} \end{matrix}\right\}$ = 3 cm.

Join G–F and H–F. See diagram for leg shaping.

For gusset shaping mark a point 10 cm along line D to A and 7 cm along line C to B; draw in gusset outline.

Notch and trace off crutch sections to make one complete section.

For Hipster Briefs

A–J = 10 cm.
A–K = 12 cm. Square across to CF from K and draw in top edge of panties.
See pattern pieces on page 121.

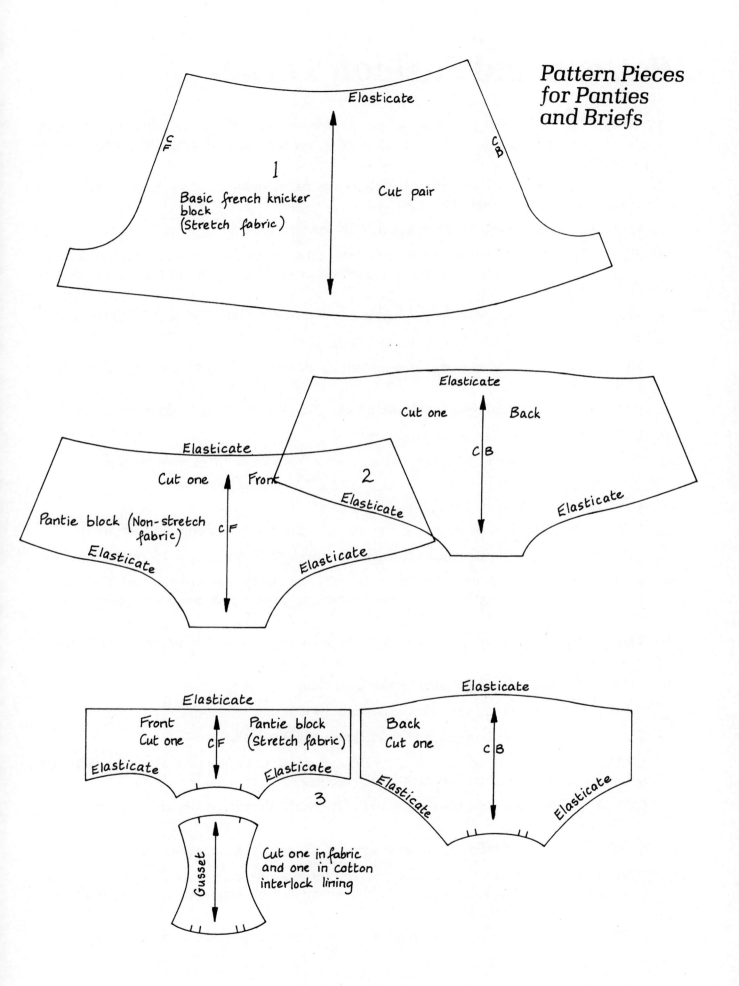

Pattern Pieces
for Panties
and Briefs

Elasticate

C F

C B

1

Basic french knicker
block
(Stretch fabric)

Cut pair

Elasticate

Elasticate

Cut one   Front   2   Back

Pantie block (Non-stretch
fabric)

Cut one

Elasticate

C F

C B

Elasticate

Elasticate

Elasticate

Elasticate

Front
Cut one   Pantie block
(Stretch fabric)

Back
Cut one

C F

C B

Elasticate

Elasticate

Elasticate

Elasticate

3

Gusset

Cut one in fabric
and one in cotton
interlock lining

Pattern and Fashion Terms

1. **BAGGING** – A method of joining facings and/or linings to the outer fabric of a garment by sewing them face to face in the form of a bag and then turning the garment to the right side.

2. **BALANCE NOTCHES** – Marks placed on seams, retaining balance and helping the machinist match the pieces in construction.

3. **BESPOKE** – Custom-made garments, usually menswear.

4. **BIAS** – The diagonal cut of the material (to obtain a true bias the material should be folded at 45° to the selvage). When a garment is bias cut it can give a soft clinging or flowing effect.

5. **BLOCK** – A cardboard master pattern used as the basis for most pattern designs.

6. **BREAK LINE** – The roll line of a turned back lapel.

7. **BUTTON STAND** – The extra amount added in pattern construction to allow for a button fastening.

8. **CANVAS** – A closely woven fabric often used as an interlining in jackets and coats.

9. **CROWN** – The shoulder area of a sleeve.

10. **DART** – A sewn shaped tuck pointed at one or both ends to remove excess material and make a garment fit.

11. **DECOLLETE** – A very low neck line.

12. **DOUBLE-FACED** – The term used for material which can be used on either side.

13. **DRAFT** – The construction plan of a garment from which the basic pattern is originated.

14. **EASE** – When one seam is fuller than the other to which it is to be joined; the excess material is evenly distributed without gathers or pleats and is then usually pressed away.

15. **FLARE** – When an amount is added into an area of a garment to enlarge it (i.e. in the hem line of a skirt).

16. **FLOUNCE OR FRILL** – A gathered strip applied to a garment.

17. **GIMP** – A special thread used for button hole stitching.

18. **GORE** – A tapered section narrower at the top; usually in skirts.

19. **GRAIN** – The direction of threads in a fabric; the straight grain (warp) is parallel to the selvage; the cross grain (weft) is at 90° to the selvage.

20. **GRAIN LINES** – Lines marked on a pattern which should be placed parallel to the selvage.

21. **GUSSET** – A piece of fabric inserted to strengthen or enlarge an area of a garment.

22. **INTERFACING** – Fabric for stiffening or reinforcing certain areas of a garment, e.g. collars, cuffs. Various kinds are available, woven or fibres matted together, and many come with a fusible finish.

23. **LAPEL** – The upper part of the front edge of a garment which folds back on to the garment.

24. MULL, MUSLIN, CALICO – Varying weights of cotton fabric used when testing patterns.

25. PEPLUM – A small hip frill at waist on bodice.

26. PILE—A surface effect on a fabric formed by tufts or loops of yarn, introduced into the fabric, i.e. velvet and corduroy. Any fabric with a pile, or a one-way print, must have all the pattern pieces cut in one direction depending on effect required. Velvet, for instance, gives a darker, more matt finish when pile is directed upwards, whilst a lighter, shinier effect is achieved when used in the opposite direction.

27. SCYE – The arm hole of a garment. Possibly derived from the words 'arms eye'.

28. STAY TAPE – A piece of tape sewn along with the seam to strengthen and/or to prevent stretching.

29. TOLERANCE – An amount added to body measurements when constructing a pattern or block. This extra amount allows for movement of the garment over a figure.

30. REGULAR FIGURE – Conforming to a recognized trade standard or type—a proportionate figure with a high percentage of occurrence in a random group.

31. WRAP – The amount by which the finished edges of a garment overlap when worn—usually with a buttoned fastening.